I SHOULD'VE HAD MY GRANDKIDS FIRST

I SHOULD'VE HAD MY GRANDKIDS FIRST

To. Papa.

E ju...

2006

ROBERT J. ADAMS

MEGAMY

The Publisher:
Megamy Publishing Ltd.
P. O. Box 3507
Spruce Grove, Alberta, Canada T7X 3A7
E-mail: megamy@interbaun.ab.ca

Library and Archives Canada Cataloguing in Publication Data
Adams, Robert J., 1938-
  I should've had my grandkids first / Robert J. Adams.

ISBN 0-9733728-2-6

1. Grandparent and child. 2. Grandparent and child–Humor
I. Title.

PN6231.G8A33 2006   306.874'5   C2006-902660-2

Senior Editor: Kelly Hymanyk
Copy Editor: Natalie King
Design, Layout and Production: Kelly Hymanyk
Cover: Nexus Design
Printing: McCallum Printing Group Inc.

CONTENTS

DEDICATION

To my granddaughters Megan and Amy

DISCLAIMER

The stories you are about to read are all true. The men, women, and children you will read about are all people from my past. I have taken the liberty of changing their names to protect their identities. Although I view the past as very humorous, they may not.

ACKNOWLEDGEMENTS

I have a very special thank you to Megan and Amy. It was their innocent, timely, and truthful comments that made the stories possible.

Thank you to Mar for once again enduring the trials of putting together another book.

Once again Natalie King has done an outstanding job of editing. Thanks to Greg Dussome for his cover design, graphics, and timely consultation.

I can never thank Kelly Hymanyk enough for all the work she put in on all phases of this endeavour. But I will try. Thank you. Thank you. Thank you.

INTRODUCTION

I Should've Had My Grandkids First, Adams' most recent collection of short stories is a charming and heartwarming look at the relationship between grandparents and their grandchildren.

After nine successful books Adams has taken on the challenge of putting into words what many grandparents feel about their own grandchildren. He enthusiastically expresses the love that is shared between the grandparent and the child while maintaining his light hearted and humorous style that has made him a favorite of the Canadian reader.

We cannot underestimate the valuable impact that grandparents have on their grandchildren. The experiences that grandparents share with their grandchildren are invaluable. There is such a short window of opportunity for these two separate generations to learn from one another. Too soon those experiences are lost forever.

You should hug your grandparents every day, even if it's only in your hearts.

MEGAMY PUBLISHING

I SHOULD'VE
HAD MY
GRANDKIDS FIRST

I SHOULD'VE HAD MY GRANDKIDS FIRST

I have often thought about the curves that are thrown at a person as he goes through life, curves that bring new challenges and change his life forever. Sometimes they even throw a person's household into a tizzy that lasts for years.

Such was the case in our lives as my wife Mar and I were catapulted into our golden years. I was about to be one of the many in Alberta to get first-hand experience in how well the downsizing game worked. Very unceremoniously I was being launched, kick-started, punted, or blasted into retirement. Downsizing was a growing trend, an epidemic that was sweeping across the land. The broom had not missed me, and I was swept up and discarded, just one among the masses.

I knew many dedicated individuals who had put

their noses to the grindstone for the company and had given the best years of their lives, only to be shunted aside in the name of progress. For a person to be pushed aside when he thought he had job security, the unknown that accompanies downsizing like a black shroud can be truly unnerving. I watched as some rebelled, fighting the trend, but to no avail; they too ended up leaving, kicking and screaming as they disappeared into the murky depths known as early retirement.

I decided that kicking and screaming while being cast aside was not for me. It was not my style. A quick goodbye, get on with the rest of my life, look for new challenges, and never look back—that was more my style. But when I received the news officially and was returning to my office for the last time, I had to wonder: What did the future hold for me?

I asked for and received two cardboard boxes. It would be my last official request of my former staff. I shut the door of my office and sat down at my desk. Slowly I pulled out one drawer at a time and scanned the contents: mostly papers, note pads, paper clips, pens and pencils. I picked out the articles that were mine—a few mementoes I had collected at various conferences across North America, items that I had brought back with me and dropped into the drawers, never to see them again until this date. My belongings didn't fill one box.

I removed the pictures from my desk—one of Mar and one double frame of my daughters, Kelly and Robin. Next came the pictures on the walls. First I removed my RCMP graduation picture: 48 Troop, 'N' Division, 1959. The graduation class from the Forestry Training School in Hinton, 1962. Half a dozen citations and plaques that I had garnered over the years. I carefully stacked these treasures in the second box.

When I finished, I sat down in my chair for the last time and looked around at what thirty-three years of dedication to a single purpose had produced: two small cardboard boxes of memories. It took me about thirty-three seconds to forget about the past thirty-three years and begin to ponder my future. I knew a person had to keep busy; however, there were no new worlds on the horizon for me to conquer. And so I prepared to meet the unknown without a single challenge. The only definite in my future was that I would meet it with Mar.

The first retirement challenge began immediately. Mar was still working, and so I inherited the role of chief cook and bottle-washer. It was a challenge that I readily accepted, although Mar seemed to be having second thoughts.

"Are you just going to sit around the house all day, or are you going to get a job?" Mar asked me. Her face had the worried look of a person who has just realized the old man is suddenly without a paycheque.

"A job?" I replied. "Who are you kidding? I've worked all my life for this moment. Now I'm going to sit back and enjoy the good life."

"You're not going to do anything?" she asked.

"Nothing," I replied, and I sat back and waited for her to respond.

"You think you're just going to sit around all day and do nothing," she said and smiled.

"That's rather a sinister smile," I remarked as I watched the worry lines disappear from her face.

"I was just thinking," she said, "as long as you've got nothing to do, you can cook. I'd like to have my supper hot and ready for me when I walk through the door."

"Really," I replied. "But you know, Mar, you might not like what I cook."

"Are you kidding?" she said and gave a hearty laugh. "I would never complain if all my meals were prepared and waiting for me everyday. I wouldn't care what you were cooking. And just think, you won't ever have to worry about being downsized again."

"You never know," I replied.

"I'm going to love this," Mar said happily.

Mar and I quickly settled into our retirement routine. I actually enjoyed cooking, and Mar was so excited; and so until something better developed, I plunged into my new role in my normal aggressive fashion. She went to work every morning and returned every evening. My days were spent doing whatever I wanted to do whenever the mood struck me. But I made sure that each day included planning a culinary delight that would please the palate of royalty. Breakfast and supper were my daily masterpieces.

On one memorable night about four months into my retirement, a night that I will never forget, I had set the table and was putting the finishing touches to our supper when Mar arrived home.

Her supper could be described as normal fare in our house since I had assumed the role of chef. We began our evening with happy hour in the family room, where we sat and talked about her day and sipped a couple of glasses of German white wine, a Riesling. Next was a bowl of homemade French onion soup with onions from my little garden. This was followed by a Caesar salad with my own special tangy dressing and anchovies. The main course consisted of very generous portions of prime-rib roast, medium rare; mashed potatoes and gravy; and, to round out the meal, buttered fresh-picked baby peas. For dessert, I had baked a Black Forest torte, which I served with an Irish coffee chaser. I do make a mean Irish coffee even if I have to say so myself. It was a meal fit for a queen. Yes, I was getting right into this retirement bit; I was having a ball and cooking up a storm.

After supper, I quickly cleaned up the dishes and then settled in on the chesterfield to watch a television show. It was a show that I had been waiting for all week, but now for the life of me I can't remember what it was even about. Mar couldn't waste her time on TV; she had a far more pressing matter on her mind. She was creating quite a racket upstairs as she sorted through her drawers and closets. Lately, for some unknown reason, she had been spending a considerable amount of time fretting about what she was going to wear to work the next day.

"I can't go on like this, if all you're going to do is stay home and cook everyday!" Mar said as she stomped down the stairs and stormed into the family room, disturbing what had been a very quiet, peaceful evening.

"Go on like what?" I asked. Her comment had caught me completely by surprise and sort of scared me. For a moment I thought she was going to suggest that I should seriously consider getting back into the workforce. I know she had mentioned on a couple of occasions lately that Safeway was hiring part-time staff.

"I can't keep eating like this every night," she said.

"Oh, is that all?" I said and gave a huge sigh of relief. "But you said you'd never complain if someone cooked all your meals for you. Didn't you?"

"Just look at me," she said, staring down at the pant suit she had on. "Look at how this suit fits me. Don't you think it's way too small on me? Don't you think I look fat?"

I knew from past experience that there was no right answer to that question. Anything I said was going to be used against me. Ever since I had known Mar, she had taken a great deal of pride in her clothes. From day one, she had been a very smart dresser and always sported the latest in fashion. She was right, though; the pantsuit which had fit her perfectly only a few weeks ago was now a little snug. In fact, the belt on the pants had almost completely disappeared under the fold that had dropped down. And the button on the jacket looked like it was spring-loaded, ready to be fired off at any moment. There was no doubt, this was a very explosive situation. It would be best, I thought, if that button popped off and hit me right between the eyes;

16

then at least I would not have to answer the question. But I had no such luck—the button held.

"You . . . you look great to me, dear. However, you could be right, that suit may be just a wee bit tight, but I doubt that anyone will notice. Do you think the dry cleaners shrank it a little?" I replied and accepted the fact that I was a coward, for I lied.

"Hmph," Mar snorted in disgust as she stormed away; up the stairs she fled, into the bedroom and slammed the door behind her. In the distance, I heard her declare, "You're no help! And for your information, clothes don't shrink when they're dry cleaned."

The next morning picked up where the evening had left off.

"Just look at me—I can't wear any of my clothes to work," Mar exclaimed as she entered the kitchen. "I've tried on every outfit that I own, and they're all the same. Everything is too tight, too small. What do you think?" she asked, referring to the latest outfit being put to the test.

Mar was decked out in a skirt and blouse, recent acquisitions to her wardrobe that she had purchased shortly after I took over the cooking duties. I remember quite well the day she brought them home and modelled them for me. If my memory served me correctly, at the time they had fit her to a T, but this morning both appeared to be a little on the snug side. Actually they were a far tighter fit than the pantsuit. Mar was bulging out all over; she sort of resembled a sausage roll.

"You look great," I said, clinging to the lie I had

begun the night before. "C'mon, sit down and have your breakfast. I've made your favourite omelette. It's got everything you like in it—bacon, mushrooms, onions, red peppers, and cheese. There's also toast, coffee, and a side order of breakfast sausages just for you."

"I told you I can't keep eating all this food, Bob," Mar said, offering only token resistance. "You're obsessed with food, you know. All this eating has got to stop."

But Mar couldn't fool me; I knew she didn't mean what she said, for as the words were coming out of her mouth, the omelette was going in. And it was a good omelette, I could tell by the look on her face. The tight clothes were forgotten for the moment.

I gave Mar a loving peck on the cheek as she waddled out the door. Now my real work began—planning the evening meal for her.

It was during that afternoon, when I was up to my elbows in brown sugar, lemons, and spices, preparing a barbecue salmon for supper, that the phone rang and everything in our lives changed forever.

"Dad, it's time! Bill is taking me to the hospital right now," Kelly said in an obvious state of panicked excitement. "Can you call Mom at work and let her know the baby is coming?"

"Consider it done! I'm on my way! I'll see you at the hospital," I warbled happily and hung up the phone.

We had been waiting for this day for the last nine months—the birth of our first grandchild. I quickly dialed up Alberta College and had Mar pulled from her

18

class. After all, this was an event that neither one of us was going to miss.

"The baby's here!" I yelled at Mar over the phone.

"Is it a little girl?" she asked. From the day we learned that we were going to be grandparents, Mar had been wishing for a girl.

"How do I know?" I replied, "Kelly just phoned and said Bill was taking her to the hospital."

"Well, the baby's not here yet, then, is it?"

"I don't know," I replied. "It could be. You know the first one can come anytime."

"Are you going to pick me up?" Mar asked.

"Nope, I'm on my way to the Royal Alex. I'll meet you there," I said. "I'm not going to be late for this for anything." And with that, I hung up the phone and bolted for the door.

I didn't waste anytime as I roared north on 170th Street and turned onto the Yellowhead Trail. Halfway between 170th Street and 156th Street, I hit the worst traffic jam I had ever seen. I had been very excited up to this point, but now I started to panic, for I realized I was in danger of being late.

"C'mon," I mumbled, "Get moving. My grandchild is going to be born any minute."

I had never seen the roads so busy in the middle of the afternoon, and it seemed to take hours until I finally arrived at 156th Street and was able to turn off the Yellowhead. I drove down to 118th Avenue, only to find that the traffic there wasn't much better, so I tried 111th Avenue. I think every vehicle in the city was on those three roads. It took forever before I finally arrived at the hospital, where it quickly became apparent that those drivers in the city who had not clogged up the roadways had taken all the parking stalls around the hospital. This trip had been a nightmare, the most miserable day of my retirement, I thought as I left my car several blocks from the hospital and sprinted for the maternity ward.

"Hi, Dad," Kelly greeted me when I burst through the door to her room.

"Where's my grandchild?" I asked, looking from Kelly to Bill to Mar. They had all arrived at the hospital ahead of me.

"We're still waiting for the stork to arrive," Mar said excitedly.

"Oh, so I guess I didn't need to rush, then, did I?"

"What took you so long, old guy?" Kelly asked.

"You're lucky you didn't come into town on the Yellowhead," I said. "I got caught up in the worst traffic jam that one person could've ever told another about."

"We came in on the Yellowhead too," she replied. "There wasn't hardly any traffic on it, was there, Bill?"

"Everything's fine," Bill replied. "Everything's fine." Ever since we found out that Kelly was pregnant, Bill had resorted to short answers. It seemed like every question was answered with the same two-word phrase, "Everything's fine."

"So, when's the baby coming?" I asked.

"When she's ready," Mar replied. After all, she was the only one in the room with experience. She was strutting as proud as a peacock in her outfit, and it was stretched out like a rubber band.

"What did the doctor say?" I asked. Being the last one in the room, I was sure that I had missed out on something important.

"My doctor hasn't arrived yet," Kelly said. "He's on holidays for two more days."

"Oh, I see. Does that mean that my grandchild has to wait until your doctor arrives?"

"No, I'll be seeing whoever is on call. Anyway, the nurse said the baby wouldn't come for a few more hours," Kelly replied.

And so we sat and waited. We stood and waited. We paced and waited. And all the time we watched a steady procession of doctors file through the delivery room. But the baby, my grandchild, didn't seem to like any of them. She was holding out for her own doctor, the one that both mother and child had become accustomed to.

Thirty-six hours later, Kelly's doctor returned from holidays. He strolled into the room as casually as if he were walking into the corner store for a soft drink on a hot day. With very little fanfare, the good doctor fired Mar and myself out of the room, where we were left to pace nervously while he welcomed the new baby into the world.

Mar and I did not pace at the same speed. She was moving quite a bit faster than I, and every time we passed in the hall she said, "Oh, I sure hope it's a little girl, don't you?"

"I hope it comes pretty soon," I finally said. "I'm getting tired."

An hour later, the distinctive sound of a newborn baby crying drifted out of the delivery room.

"She's here!" Mar shouted excitedly and raced towards the door.

"Wait, you can't go in there until the doctor says you can," a nurse said as she moved to head Mar off—although she did pause for a second, unsure if she wanted to step in front of the determined lady in the tight-fitting outfit.

"What do you mean, I can't go in there," Mar said, demanding an explanation.

"When the baby is ready to receive visitors, the doctor will come out and tell you," the nurse replied.

The crying stopped, and Mar and I continued to pace.

"I hope it's a girl," Mar repeated for the umpteenth time.

It seemed to be hours before the doctor finally came out of the delivery room.

"Are you people the grandparents?" he asked.

"We are," I replied.

"Oh, I hope it's a girl," Mar said.

"Well, why are you standing around out here?" the doctor asked. "Why didn't you come in and meet your grandchild?"

Mar blew past both of us and burst into the room. I was right on her heels. Bill was standing beside the bed holding the baby.

"It's a girl," he said, several times. He had added three words to his vocabulary.

"It's a girl," Mar warbled happily as she scooped the baby out of Bill's arms. "We've got our little girl."

And so the first challenge of retirement was eclipsed. As Mar stood there bulging out of her outfit, food was forgotten; it had been replaced by grandparenthood — which, in hindsight, is much more satisfying, and calorie-free. Our lives have never been the same since our grandchildren were born. I'm sure this is what life was always intended to be. As I look back, I do believe I should've had my grandkids first.

"SORRY, OLD GUY."

When we were about to go to press with this book it was brought to my attention that there was no mention of the birth of my second grandchild, Amy. After all, I had gone into great detail describing Megan's birth. It was certainly not that I overlooked this important day, as it was just as exciting and monumental in my grandparenting journey as the first birth.

I can remember the day as if it were yesterday. The birth of our second grandchild was near and I had taken Kelly for her check up. I was helping with Megan while Kelly was in the doctors office. It was during this checkup that the first signs of labour appeared. I, being the dutiful grandfather, whisked her and Megan over to the hospital where I stayed with them until Bill and a very excited Nanna arrived. If it was possible, Nanna was even more excited this time and kept repeating, "Oh, I hope it's a girl!"

Now, I fully expected that Nanna would want to take Megan home and look after her until Kelly and baby arrived home. I would be left to pace the corridor in the hospital alone. But alas, I was mistaken. What a foolish assumption on my part.

Unbeknownst to me, there had been a little skullduggery going on when I wasn't around. Yes, Kelly and Nanna had made a plan. Formed a pact you might say. Nanna was going to be with Kelly in the delivery room for baby number two.

"Sorry, old guy," Kelly said, "but this is really a woman thing.

"I understand," I said. Then I dressed Megan for a ride home, where I would pace the floor waiting for the phone call.

No, I wasn't at the hospital when Amy was born and Nanna was so excited, that she forgot to phone me. It wasn't until Bill and Nanna arrived home in the wee hours of the morning that I learned about the birth of my second grandchild. It was a little girl.

THE BABYSITTERS

"Guess what, Pa," Nanna warbled happily. (Mar and I had settled nicely into our new role as "Nanna" and "Pa" since Megan arrived in our lives.)

Nanna was so excited that she was literally bouncing, hardly able to contain the great news. I knew it had to be something extra special. Something that was giving her a great deal of pleasure. I had absolutely no idea what could possibly have occurred that would put her in such a great frame of mind, but I took a stab at it anyway.

"Your mother is coming to visit," I ventured. I knew her mother wasn't travelling all that much anymore, but there were very few things in this world that put Nanna in such a great frame of mind.

"Guess again," she said, and her happy tone did not change. "It's something even better."

"Hmm, even better than your mother coming! Wow,

that has to be something really special," I said. I tried to think of what it could be, but I kept drawing blanks. "I'm sorry, Nanna, I have absolutely no idea what it could be. I guess you're going to have to help me."

"Aw c'mon, *Pa*, don't be a party-pooper," she said, putting a big emphasis on *Pa*. "Take another guess."

"All right, let me see... ah, I got it, we won the lotto, right?" Then I shrugged my shoulders. "I don't know, Nanna. Why don't you just tell me."

"Kelly and Bill are going to Mexico," she said. "Isn't that wonderful?"

"What? Wha-what do you mean? Don't tell me they—they're moving to Mexico," I sputtered. I could hardly believe what I was hearing. I mean, both of them are teachers, and it was not uncommon for teachers to take a year or two and teach in another country. But Mexico? "I don't see what's so great about that!"

"No, silly," she replied and laughed. "They're going to Mexico on a week's holiday."

"Don't scare me like that," I said. "But just a minute, I thought they had to teach. How can they get time off during the school year to go to Mexico?"

"They're going over spring break," she said, "and we're going to babysit the girls! We get to have Megan and Amy all to ourselves for a whole week," she said, and her voice was alive with excitement.

"Well now, that is great news, Nanna," I said. "No, actually it's better than great—it's wonderful. Just think, a whole week with the girls, and there'll be no one around to tell us what we're doing wrong or how we should be doing things. How will we ever survive?"

"Oh, I'm so excited, I can hardly wait, I'm going to spoil them rotten!" Nanna warbled happily.

"Me too," I said.

At that moment I couldn't think of a better way to spend my golden years than with my granddaughters, two beautiful little girls, aged one and three. To be sure, there is nothing in this world that I would rather do.

Long before spring break arrived, Nanna had packed and repacked the few things that she was sure we would need. By the time spring break arrived and I finished packing the suitcases, bags, and boxes into our minivan, I was certain that she was taking half of our household. There was barely enough room left for Nanna in the van as we began the twenty-six-kilometre trek to Spruce Grove.

"You're very quiet. You must be really excited?" I said to Nanna as we sped west on Highway 16. Since this was our first real opportunity to have our granddaughters to ourselves for an extended period of time, I couldn't wait to hear once more how excited Nanna was, even though she didn't appear to be herself.

"I think I'm coming down with the flu," she replied, and there was no joy in her voice. "I don't feel very good."

"Really! Well, you look okay to me," I said, hoping to cheer her up and get her mind off this sudden illness. "You're probably just over excited."

"I've got the chills, my throat is sore, and I've got a headache," she said in a voice that sounded so sad and forlorn.

"C'mon Nanna, cheer up. You'll feel better as soon as you see the girls," I said.

But she didn't.

No one was able to cheer Nanna up: not Kelly; not Megan or Amy, who both raced to the door to meet us, squealing with delight; not even Spunky, the little black poodle that she loved. These were all sure signs that Nanna was under the weather and going down for the count.

"Is Mom okay?" Kelly asked me after taking one look at Nanna. "She doesn't look very good." To say that Nanna looked like death warmed over would have been a compliment to her.

"She's fine," I lied. "She's just excited. I think she's got herself too worked up. I'm sure she'll be fine in the morning."

"I've put clean sheets on the bed in our bedroom," Kelly advised long before it was time to turn in for the night.

"That's okay," I replied. "You sleep in your own bed and get a good night's sleep before you embark on your journey."

"Well, no, Dad," she replied, somewhat surprised. "I thought you would like to sleep in our room—its all ready for you."

"No-no, that's all right, Kelly," Nanna croaked in a feeble voice. "You sleep in your own bed. I'll just sleep in the spare bed in the basement."

"No you won't. I want you to sleep upstairs. I told Megan that you would be in our bed when she gets up in the morning, and if you're not there, she might get scared."

"She won't be scared," I scoffed. "I'm sure she's used to seeing you and Bill in your bed when she gets up in the morning. Isn't she?"

"Ya, but we'll be on a plane when she wakes up, and you need to be sleeping in our bed. I told Megan you would be in our bed, and you'll be in our bed when she comes in in the morning," Kelly stated emphatically. "Oh, and by the way, Dad, could you set the alarm and call me at three.?"

"Right," I said, "but why do we have to get up at three a.m.? What time does your flight leave anyway?"

"At six, but we've got to leave here by four — and in case you forgot, old guy, you're driving us to the airport."

At three a.m. sharp I quietly snuck downstairs and found a chair beside the kitchen table, where I crashed and sat like a zombie.

"Jeeez Dad, do you ever look tired! Don't tell me you're coming down with the flu too?" Kelly asked as she strode into the room bright-eyed and bushy-tailed.

"I'm fine. Slept like a baby," I replied. "I always look this was at three in the morning."

"Speaking of babies, how did my babies sleep?" she asked. "Did they wake you up?"

"Did they wake me up? Naw!" I said, but that wasn't really true.

*   *   *   *   *

I was out like a light, dead to the world, as soon as my head hit the pillow. However, a short time later I was jolted back to the world of the living. A piercing, blood-curdling scream cut through the quiet of the night like a knife.

"What was that?" I shouted as I sat bolt upright in bed, trying desperately to get my bearings. "Where are we?" Everything around me was foreign, and my heart was pounding wildly in my chest, creating a rush of blood to my head.

"We're in Kelly's bed," Nanna replied, her gravelly voice no more than a whisper.

"What are we doing in Kelly's bed?" I asked, forgetting where we were and what we were doing.

"We're babysitting, remember."

"Oh yeah, right. What on earth was that horrible scream?"

"It's only Amy, now go back to sleep. I've got a headache and you're making it worse," Nanna said.

"That can't be Amy!" I said. "It sounded as if somebody was being killed."

"Go back to sleep," Nanna replied.

"Is—is she okay?" I asked?.

"I told you, she's fine," Nanna groaned. "Please let me go back to sleep."

"How come she screamed like that?" I said. "That isn't normal. You better go in and check on her. It sounds to me like she's crying."

"Kelly said they don't consider that to be crying. Sometimes Amy will let out a little scream in her sleep, that's all. She's fine, go back to sleep," Nanna said and rolled over to go back to sleep herself.

"How do you feel?" I asked, hoping that her health was improving.

"Horrible."

I lay there in the dark, listening, but all was quiet. There was no more screaming, no more noises that only sounded like crying, so I rolled over and closed my eyes and listened to my heart still beating like a trip-hammer. But sleep would not come. I lay there with my eyes closed, praying that I could fall back to sleep.

I was somewhere between groggy and drowsy, listening for another scream, when a horrible, eerie feeling came over me. That scream I had heard a few minutes before was not normal. Something was wrong. I knew it. In the darkness, I could feel the hair on the back of my neck standing on end. Then my sixth sense told me that Nanna and I were not alone in this room. I had this uncomfortable feeling that out of the night there were eyes staring at me. It was the feeling people get when they sense they're being watched. And right now I knew I was being watched.

Slowly I opened one eye, and my pounding heart just about stopped beating. There before my eyes, at the edge of the bed, standing over me, was an intruder. It was a ghostly white intruder with a sheet draped over its head. For a moment I couldn't move, I could only lie there helplessly and stare at the image that was hovering over me. It was just there, not moving, not speaking, only staring back at me.

Finally the sheet moved, and I breathed a sigh of relief when I realized it wasn't a ghost—it was Megan. She was clutching her blankie, her snow-white blankie, tightly to her little chest. She stood there silently while my heart gradually began beating again.

"Hi, buddy," I said weakly. "Would you like to sleep with Nanna and Pa?"

"I have to go to the bathroom," she said.

"Okay, you can go to the bathroom, then," I said

"Okay, Pa," she replied and raced out of the bedroom.

A groggy fog quickly enveloped me and I faintly recall a little person crawling over me. She dragged her blankie across me and instantly fell sound asleep.

Some time later, after I had fallen asleep, I had a sudden feeling that I was at the edge of a crowd standing near the lip of a cliff. The crowd was moving slowly, and I was being forced over the cliff. I woke up in a panic, sweating profusely and thrashing about wildly before I realized that I wasn't at the lip of a cliff, but on the edge of the bed, and I was on the verge of crashing to the floor.

I reached over my head and grabbed onto the mattress in my struggle to stay on the bed. Then I became aware of the little person with the blankie — she had turned sideways in the bed. Both of her little feet were set in my ribs and she was exerting just enough pressure to force me to move. I struggled to maintain a toehold and stay on the bed without waking her.

Suddenly another piercing screech erupted from the room down the hall. I lost my grip on the mattress, rolled off the bed, and landed on the floor. Amy was once more performing an excellent imitation of crying. This time the illusion carried on for an extended period of time and bordered on the real thing. Now, I'm no expert on the subject of baby-howling in the middle of the night, but I know that if this screech had been considered real crying, it would have been heard in the basement, and that either Mommy or Daddy or both would have come running. But there was no movement, no sound from those quarters. Megan didn't even wince, and Nanna appeared to be sound asleep.

I got up off the floor, rearranged the little person so that there was once more room for three in the bed, and crawled back in. I lay there, trying to convince myself that the screech was not real. But I guess I must have been wrong and the screech was genuine. Finally Nanna could take it no longer, and she bolted from her side of the king-size bed, grumbling incoherently.

"Where are you going?" I asked.

"My throat's so sore, I can hardly swallow," she proclaimed as she stumbled towards Amy's room.

This show of activity was enough for Amy, for she abruptly quit imitating a good crying jag, and Nanna only moaned as she groped her way back to bed. I was wide awake, but I closed my eyes and tried to sleep. Sleep was slow in coming, but finally I drifted off. . . only to once again wake up with a start.

I could sense that something was wrong, but I was having difficulty putting my finger on it. Then it dawned on me. It was the pressure on my ribs from the little feet. It was missing. Oh, the little feet were there all right, but the pressure was gone. I reached over and gently touched one foot, but it was lifeless. I held my breath and listened for the sound of her breathing. I

35

couldn't detect any sign of life. The first thought that entered my head was that I had rolled on Megan and she was not breathing.

"Megan," I whispered. Nothing. I could feel the panic set in.

"Megan," I said out loud and shook her. Too late I realized that I had just committed the cardinal sin: I had woken a sleeping baby.

Instantly she was wide awake and alert. As if it was time to get up. Now she wanted to talk.

"Go to sleep, buddy," I mumbled. "It's not time to get up."

"Pa," came the quiet little voice.

"Yes, buddy," I replied.

"I want to show you something."

"What do you want to show me."

"Uhhh, something," she replied, searching for what that something might be.

"Please, go to sleep, buddy," I replied and tried to bury my head in the pillow.

"Tickle my back, Pa?" she asked.

"Go to sleep," I whispered and rolled over to reclaim my edge of the bed.

"Mommy always tickles my back and then I can go back to sleep," Megan informed me. And so I rubbed her little back.

There was no need to have worried about setting the alarm clock. I was wide awake at three a.m. when the alarm barely broke the silence of the night.

Strange, I thought. The alarm was turned down low so it wouldn't wake the girls—and it didn't—but it

36

woke the two sleeping in the basement. They were the same two who hadn't heard the nighttime antics that had been a steady performance all night.

*   *   *   *   *

"Are you sure you're okay, Dad?" Kelly asked me again. She looked wide awake, relaxed and rested, ready for her holiday.

"Oh, me, absolutely, I'm fine. Slept like a baby," I lied.

"Can I get you something?" she asked. "Would you like me to make you some breakfast?"

"Na," I faked a smile. "I'm fine lets just go. I don't want to wake the girls. I'll get a bite to eat at the airport. Once you're checked in, then we can sit down and relax. I'll treat you to breakfast."

"Okay. Give me five and I'll be ready to go," she said.

Traffic between Spruce Grove and the Edmonton International Airport is really light at three-thirty a.m. It was a cloudless night and the sky was studded with stars. Bill pointed out Comet Hale-Bop, which was now racing through the northern skies. I never would have seen it without his help.

"Isn't it interesting," I said, "the comet seems to have reversed directions and is now moving to the northeast.

"No way," replied Kelly.

"Well, look for yourself," I replied. "I distinctly remember I looked at the comet the other night, and the tail was pointing to the east; and this morning it's pointing towards the southwest." I mean, anybody with

37

any sense of direction could see the obvious change.

"The comet's tail always points away from the sun." Bill pointed out this scientific tidbit.

"Oh yeah, right," I mumbled.

*   *   *   *   *

"Enjoy your flight and your breakfast on the plane," I said when I learned that the only restaurant at the airport was closed and wouldn't open until six a.m.

"Oh, and another thing before I forget, Dad — remember when you feed Spunky, she only gets dog food. She gets sick if you feed her anything else."

"I don't know why, we always fed our dogs table scraps and they never got sick," I replied. "Fang even ate sauerkraut, and it never bothered her."

"Do what you want, old guy," Kelly said, "but don't say I didn't warn you."

"We'll be fine," I said. "After all, we did raise you, remember."

"And if Mom isn't feeling any better, would you take the girls for a walk every day —"

"Bye, Kell," I said. "Enjoy your holiday. And don't worry, I promise, we'll look after Megan and Amy."

*   *   *   *   *

And the week passed. I'm sure Kelly was surprised to see me at the airport still alive and in far better shape than when she last saw me.

"Hi, Daddy, how are my babies?" It was the first question out of Kelly's mouth as she walked through the doors coming out of Canada Customs at the Edmonton International Airport.

"They're fine. In fact, they're doing so well, they

probably won't even remember you," I said and laughed.

"How's Nanna?" Kelly asked.

"She's still under the weather," I said "but I think she's started to feel a little better."

"Is she still sick?"

"Yup, she's still sick."

"Well, I hope you didn't stay in the house the whole time. Please tell me you took the girls out for some fresh air?" Kelly asked, and there was no missing the concern in her eyes.

"Every day," I replied. "Among other things, I made sure I took them for at least a walk every day."

*   *   *   *   *

From the first day to the last day, Megan, Amy, and I went for an invigorating walk along the streets of Spruce Grove. Both girls and myself needed to walk out a few kinks and get some fresh air. Nanna, who loves to walk more than anybody, held down the fort. Mostly she slept, trying to shake the flu.

We quickly settled into a walking routine. I had decided that for our week, we would spend as little time in the house as possible. I was determined to spend good quality time with my granddaughters. Quality time would start each morning with a nice brisk walk. Every morning, right after breakfast, I would bundle up the girls. I tucked Amy snugly into her stroller; Megan, who was walking, chose to hold onto the stroller rather than Pa's hand.

"When do we get back to my house?" Megan would ask before we had walked the distance from the driveway to the sidewalk on the other side of the street.

"Well, buddy, we've just started," I would reply, "but we'll come back to the house as soon as we've got some fresh air."

"I've already got some fresh air, Pa," she would advise me.

"Well, Pa and Amy need a little more fresh air, buddy," I would say.

"I don't want to walk no more, Pa," Megan would say about the time we reached the sidewalk. "I'm too tired."

"Are you sure you're tired, buddy?" I would ask her.

"I can't walk anymore."

It was the spring of the year and it seemed as if there was always a seagull or two either flying overhead or picking at a morsel along the road.

"Look at the birdie," I would say, trying to get her mind on something else. "Do you know what kind of bird that is, Megan?"

"I'm really tired, Pa," she would say, ignoring me.

"It sure looks like a seagull to me. Does it look like a seagull to you?"

"My legs are tired. I can't walk anymore," she would say and stop walking. Obviously this poor little girl was suffering.

"Do you have to walk when you go with Mommy?" I asked.

"Uh-huh," Megan replied. "I have to walk all the way."

"Well, you certainly don't have to walk all the way when you're with Pa," I said. "C'mon, buddy, Pa will carry you." And then I'd scoop her up in my arms and hoist her onto my shoulders. There, she could get a much better look at the countryside and the birds.

"What kind of bird is that?" Megan would ask as she rode along with her little hands clutched over my forehead. It was as if she had just discovered the seagull.

"I think it's a seagull. Should we see if we can find some more?"

"Okay, Pa." Then after some serious deliberation, she would ask. "How come Nanna doesn't have to go for a walk?"

"Nanna's sick," I would say. "We'll have to let her sleep so she can get better." Megan always had a million questions after she was given the prime seat, where she could have walked forever.

*   *   *   *   *

"And my puppy. How's my Spunky?" Kelly asked.

"Oh, Spunky is just fine, too," I said. "And when we fed her, we only gave her dog food, just as you wanted.

*   *   *   *   *

Actually that wasn't entirely true. There were a couple of incidents.

One day, after our walk, I realized something was missing as soon as we walked through the door. Spunky, the little black poodle, should have been there to bark up a storm and greet us, but she was missing. I checked the stuffed donut that was her bed. No dog lying there. I knew she had to be in the house

41

somewhere, as the only way out would have been through the crack under the door. But where?

While I was busy getting Amy out of her walking clothes, Megan kicked off her boots, hung her coat on the floor to prevent it from falling down, and took off. Like magic, she was not tired and her legs did not hurt anymore. I was surprised at the speed with which she raced off to check on Nanna.

"Pa! Pa!" Megan screamed from the living room.

That screech succeeded in getting Nanna's attention as well as mine. Nanna dragged herself out of bed and thumped her way downstairs. She arrived on the scene about the same time as I did. Nanna looked as if she was about to collapse.

Megan stood in the living room on Kelly's nice, new, off-white rug. She was pointing to a huge, brown, creamy, gooey, messy mass of partly digested chocolate. Steam rose from the mess, and the perimeter spread as the deposit slowly oozed out across the off-white rug.

Meanwhile Spunky, trying desperately to be inconspicuous, was departing the scene of the disaster. She had her tail tucked tightly between her legs, her belly hugging the floor like a snake as she slithered towards the safety of the kitchen.

"What's that, Pa?" Megan asked, not taking her eyes off the ever-expanding mess.

"Looks to me like Spunky has found a stash of chocolate goodies and has left us a little present," I said. For the steaming, spreading mess was none other then a huge amount of chocolate that Spunky had obviously first devoured and then regurgitated onto the off-white rug, where it would be easiest to see.

"Ohhhh," commented Amy, who could not yet speak, as she pursed her little lips and pointed one tiny finger at the chocolate to show that she too had seen the dog's contribution to our babysitting efforts.

"Did someone feed Spunky some chocolate?" I asked. In our house, whenever I use the term *someone*, it usually means Nanna.

"Oh no!" Nanna groaned and hobbled, as fast as her wobbly legs would allow, over to the door. "I bought some Easter eggs for the girls, and I must have left them at the door. Look, I did," she said picking up a handful of badly mangled and torn Easter-egg wrappers from among the many bags and boxes that had been piled just inside the door when we first arrived.

"Is Spunky in trouble, Pa?" Megan asked when I picked Spunky up and carried her over to the door.

"No, buddy, it's not Spunky's fault. I'm just going to put her out in case she gets sick again.

"You take the girls into the kitchen," Nanna moaned, "and I'll handle this."

"C'mon girls, let's go into the kitchen," I said as I quickly guided them both out of the danger zone.

"Why do we got to go into the kitchen?" Megan complained.

"Because Pa's going to make you some hot chocolate. After that good refreshing walk, you probably need some hot chocolate, don't you?"

"Can you put whipped cream and a cherry on top like Mom does?" Megan asked.

"I sure can, buddy," I replied.

"I don't like hot chocolate if there's no cherry on top," she said.

"Okay, two hot chocolates with whipped cream and cherries on top, coming up!"

Two days later we had our second incident.

Amy was enjoying her afternoon nap, and Nanna was in bed, still trying to shake the flu.

"Pa," Megan said to me as she and I were settling down on the chesterfield to watch a *Barney* episode on television.

"Yes, buddy," I said.

"What's that, Pa?"

I looked over to where she was pointing, and there on the rug I could see two little piles. They resembled two stacks of wrinkled red marbles.

"I don't know," I replied. "What does it look like to you?"

"It looks like dog poop!" she exclaimed.

"It can't be, buddy. Dog poop's not red." I chuckled and got up to have a closer look.

"Is it dog poop, Pa?" she asked.

"No buddy, it's . . . it's cherries!" I turned and faced the upstairs bedroom. "Nanna, how did cherries get down here on the rug?" I roared to make sure she heard me. However, the lack of response told me that either she hadn't heard me or was fast asleep.

Then a movement against the far wall caught my eye. There was Spunky, and once more she was slinking from the room with her tail between her legs.

"Is it dog poop?" Megan asked.

"No, buddy, I do believe it's vomit," I replied. "And it looks like Spunky has eaten some cherries, and she's thrown up on the rug again."

"Nanna, where did Spunky get the cherries?" I bellowed at the stairs a second time. This time I had more success in communicating with the sick.

"Oh no," Nanna groaned. Her voice was cracking. "I forgot that I had bought some chocolate-covered cherries for the girls when I got the Easter eggs. I must have left them by the door too."

*   *   *   *   *

"Did my babies miss me?" Kelly asked.

"I don't know," I replied. "I never asked them and they didn't say."

"Did they eat okay?"

"Did they eat okay? You betcha! I think that they ate everything in sight. They're real little troopers when it comes to eating. I even took them out for supper one night."

"And how did that go?"

"Fantastic," I replied. "Absolutely fantastic. It was an unforgettable experience."

*   *   *   *   *

Well, that wasn't exactly accurate either, although I must say I won't soon forget the evening.

Megan and Amy were in a great mood. They had had a great day, and Spunky had given us a day without finding a stash of chocolate. Even Nanna seemed to be shaking off the effects of the flu and said she was feeling a little better. I offered to treat everyone to supper that night. Megan got to choose the

45

restaurant. We travelled into Edmonton to the restaurant of her choice, where we were shown to the only table available, a nice quiet spot near the back of the restaurant. It quickly became apparent why it was still available — it just happened to be right next to the washrooms. I avoided looking up after my first glance revealed that I had the best view into the ladies' washroom.

Amy decided that eating at this particular restaurant was not really that high on her list of priorities. Long before our food arrived she arched her little back and, much to the annoyance of those sitting around us, announced her displeasure at having her highchair in the aisle, where every person going to the bathroom seemed to bump into it. Of course, since she couldn't speak, we couldn't be sure about the source of the displeasure-whether it was the restaurant, the constant bumping, or pizza aroma mingling the various odours emanating from the washrooms that she was objecting to. But the body language told us that she was certainly objecting. Everything we put on her highchair — crayons, colouring paper, and spoons — had all been quickly flung to the floor.

Finally Nanna found her something to her liking. It was the two dishes holding the sugar packs and the creamers that calmed her down. She was quite happy as she occupied herself by taking all the sugar packs out of the dish and then putting them back in, one at a time. The creamers she stacked one on top of the other, making a little castle. Our neighbours smiled their approval at this sudden pleasant change of events.

Some even commented, "How sweet!"

Suddenly, without any warning, Amy decided she wanted to be a ball player, a pitcher no less. Creamers and packets of sugar began to fly around the room. A lady two booths down flinched and ducked as a packet of sugar landed squarely in her plate of ravioli. The gentleman with her was kind enough to pick it out of her plate and return it to Amy. He plunked it down on the highchair tray without so much as a word. I snatched it up quickly, not wanting my granddaughter to soil her little jumpsuit with ravioli sauce.

Finally our food was delivered. Amy had the child's portion of spaghetti. Megan had Dino Fingers. Nanna had chosen the Thai Salad and I opted for the Greek Salad.

"Can I have your olives, Pa?" Megan asked me.

"Absolutely," I replied, a little taken aback. "I didn't know you liked olives."

"I eat olives all the time," she replied, so I picked them out of my salad and put them in the basket with her Dino Fingers and fries.

I was pleasantly surprised as I watched her insert one little finger into the hole in each of the pitted black olives.

"Megan, are you sure you like to eat olives?" I asked.

"Uh-huh," she said. "I really like olives."

Then, as Nanna and I watched in silence, she carefully picked the olives off her fingers one at a time with her lips, and ate every one.

"You sure do like olives, don't you, buddy?" I said, praising her.

"Can I have more olives, Pa?" she asked.

"Absolutely, buddy," I replied. "I'll get you some more right now." And with that, I hailed the waitress over to our table.

The waitress arrived back at the table with Megan's olives about the same time as Amy decided she was finished with her spaghetti and flipped her plate over the side of the highchair, where it splattered over the floor. The waitress, who had been moving at snail speed all evening, was actually very nimble. She showed some fancy footwork and catlike quickness in avoiding flying spaghetti, splattering sauce, and shards of shattered plate.

*   *   *   *   *

"If Mom was sick most of the time, who looked after my babies?" Kelly asked.

"We both did," I replied.

"And did you change diapers, or did Mom have to get up and do that?"

"I did," I said. "It was a piece of cake."

"Yeah, right," Kelly said, like she didn't believe me.

"I admit that I was a little rusty in that department, but I think I managed okay," I said.

*   *   *   *   *

Actually, the first time I changed the diaper was a little dicey.

"What can I do now, Pa?" Megan asked, indicating she was tired of watching the golf game on the television.

48

"What would you like to do, buddy?"

"I don't know. What can I do?"

"I think I've got a job for you, Megan—how would you like to help Pa?" I asked her.

"Okay," she replied happily.

"How would you like to get Pa a diaper from the change table?" I asked.

"Why do you need a diaper?" she asked.

"Because it smells like it's time to change Amy's diaper," I said.

"But Pa, Nanna always changes Amy's diaper," she said.

"I know, buddy, but Nanna is sick, so Pa will change it this time." After Nanna's bout with the dog chocolate on the off-white rug, I figured she didn't need any more activity. Anyway, I didn't feel that it was necessary to wake her for this menial task.

"Okay, Pa, I'll get the diaper."

"That's a good girl," I said.

"Here, Pa," Megan said when she returned from upstairs with the diaper. She proudly held the Pamper up for inspection, quite proud that she had been a big help.

"Thanks, buddy," I said, praising her. "You're sure Pa's big helper, aren't you?"

"Uh-huh," she replied, and proceeded to balance herself on the arm of the chesterfield to watch the performance.

"Be careful you don't fall, buddy," I cautioned her as I flipped Amy over onto her back on the chesterfield and prepared to peel off the soiled diaper.

Amy, however, had other thoughts. She always seemed to rise to the challenge whenever she was changed. The second her back hit the chesterfield, she protested: immediately she arched her little back and began to scream like she was being beaten. Undaunted, I held her down and proceeded with the task.

Soiled diaper! I didn't know the half of it. It was more than soiled. It was a diaper so full of caca, the likes of which had not been seen in years. It was the mother load. Now I had a problem. I had a kid screaming her head off, twisting and turning like a bucking Brahma bull, thrashing around on the chesterfield, her butt covered with caca. I needed wipes, but I had forgotten to get them. I needed help. Once more, I needed Megan.

"Megan," I tried to smile at her and keep the caca from being spread all over the chesterfield, the way the chocolate had been on the rug. "Would you be a good girl, and go and get me the wipes, please?"

"I can't. I don't know how," she replied, still balancing herself delicately on the arm of the chesterfield.

"Sure you do, buddy," I encouraged her. "They're on the change table, in the same place where you got the diaper."

"But I can't," she protested. "I don't know how."

"Please," I coaxed.

"It stinks in here!" she declared, and promptly forgot about the balancing act. Then she calmly walked over to the other side of the room and proceeded to find something more interesting and less smelly to do.

Meanwhile Amy and I were having a real wrestling

50

match. She had her little mouth wide open and was screaming bloody murder. Her little arms and legs were flailing wildly in a desperate attempt to escape. I was just as desperate. I was hanging on to her for dear life as caca was coming precariously close to being splattered and smeared all over me and the chesterfield.

A thump on the floor from the bedroom overhead told me that Nanna had heard the commotion and, as sick as she was, was coming to the rescue.

*   *   *   *   *

"Was everything really okay, Dad? You know, I worry about you old people."

Did we make out okay? Suddenly I had myriad flashbacks that scrolled through my head. I had completely forgotten what it was like to have little people in the house. I know there was a time when I figured it would be impossible to forget the many sleepless nights I had experienced with our own girls when they were small. How many nights had I lain awake or hovered over the crib when they were babies, listening and watching for a sign that they were still breathing? Far too many to count.

I had forgotten there was never any downtime. From the minute the kids awoke until they finally fell asleep at the end of the day, they required attention. Attention that we happily provided. And even when they didn't need or want attention, it was given readily.

Oh yes, and who could ever forget the endless stream of pets that had had the run of our house along with the children? I had forgotten, or at least it seemed as if I had; however, it only took one little black poodle,

51

Spunky, to bring back a flood of memories. The little indiscreet messages that Spunky dropped on the rug were reminiscent of the many gifts from the countless pets that had come before—the most memorable of these pets being the cat that chose to use my toe rubbers as her sandbox.

Why, I had even misplaced the memories of the baby responsibilities that made such a dramatic impact on me many years ago. The baby responsibilities came racing back into my mind with the reintroduction to the diaper full of caca. Once more I knew my sense of smell was keen and my gagging reflexes were still working quite well, thank you.

"Did we make out okay, you ask, Kelly? Absolutely. The girls were real little dolls. Everything went like clockwork; there was not even so much as a hiccup the whole week. In fact, we can't wait for your next holiday, so that Nanna and I can babysit again."

THE DISCOVERY ZONE

"I need a break," I said in a moment of weakness. It was a slip of the tongue and spoken in a voice that was a little louder than I had intended. "I have to get out of the house for a while. I think I'm going crazy."

Once more Mar and I were babysitting our granddaughters Megan and Amy. And once more Nanna was down with the flu. We had been housebound for three days, and Pa was beginning to wear down.

"I know where we can go when you're going crazy, Pa," three-year-old Megan said, and I could just feel the enthusiasm in her voice.

"Do you, buddy?" I said, and smiled. Obviously "I think I'm going crazy" was an expression she had heard before.

"Uh-huh, I do, Pa," she said. Even though her voice had turned very serious, there was a twinkle in her eye.

"And just where would we go when Pa is going crazy, buddy?" I asked.

"We could all go to the Discovery Zone," she said, and the excitement was building.

"The Discovery Zone," I said, and I looked to Nanna for help. I had never heard of the Discovery Zone.

"I think that's a good idea," Nanna said. Her input was absolutely no help at all.

"What is the Discovery Zone?" I asked.

"Get with the program, Pa," Nanna said, laughing. "Everybody knows what the Discovery Zone is.

"Yeah, Pa. Everybody knows what the Discovery Zone is," Megan said.

"Well no, buddy, everybody doesn't know what the Discovery Zone is. Pa doesn't know," I said, feeling a little foolish.

"I do, Pa," Megan said, and once more her voice was very serious.

"Okay then, who's going to tell Pa what the Discovery Zone is, and where do we find it?"

"It's where you play games, Pa," Megan said. "There's slides and there's tubes to crawl through and there's blocks. Me and you could have lots of fun," Megan said, and her eyes were dancing with excitement.

"Well, that sure sounds like fun, buddy," I said. "But what would Amy do while you and I were having all this fun? I think she's just a wee bit too little to do all those fun things."

"No, Pa, Amy likes to go to the Discovery Zone too. There's this one place that's full of plastic balls and Amy likes to sit in the balls and throw them around," Megan said. "She just needs someone to sit with her."

"Well, I guess I could sit with Amy and throw balls," I said. "Pa's a pretty good ball-thrower, you know."

"No, Pa, you have to play with me," Megan said. "Nanna has to sit with Amy."

"I'm not sure how that will work, buddy. You know Nanna has the flu and she's not feeling very good."

"I'm fine," Nanna chimed in, her croaky voice cracking under the strain.

"You don't look so fine," I replied. "You look like you've just been dragged through a knothole."

"I won't feel any better lying around here," Nanna said and gave me a nasty look. "I might just as well go to the Discovery Zone."

"You know, buddy, someone is going to have to tell me how to get to the Discovery Zone, because Pa doesn't know where it is."

"I do, Pa, I know where it is. I'll show you how to get there."

And she did; she knew exactly where to go to help keep Pa from going crazy. By the time we arrived, Nanna looked like death warmed over. I wasn't sure that she was going to make the trek about fifty feet from the car to the Discovery Zone.

"C'mon Pa!" yelled Megan as she raced ahead.

"Are you okay?" I asked Nanna.

"I told you, I'm fine," she replied.

"You have to pay here, Pa," Megan said, standing at the counter and waiting for me to dig deep.

I was dumbfounded as I stood looking around the inside of the Discovery Zone. The place was huge. I noticed an area set aside for the very little kids where there was a section full of baseball-sized plastic balls. This, I thought, would be a good place for Nanna and Amy. A place where Nanna could sit and Amy could play, where she wouldn't get lost and also would be away from the danger of being bowled over by bigger kids.

To the right was the real discovery zone—here were the hanging dummies, the tunnels, the slides, and all sorts of climbing apparatus for youngsters. The cafeteria, off to the left, was not lost on me. It was crowded with parents, some sitting and watching, some sitting and reading, some sitting and visiting. I would be a watcher, I concluded as I handed the attendant our entrance fee.

"Okay, Megan, get in there and do some jumping and running and sliding," I said when the tab had been cleared.

"You can't go in here like that, Pa," Megan the rule-follower informed me. "You have to take off your coat and your shoes. You can't play in here with your shoes on!"

"Right," I replied. "It was a test, buddy. You go on ahead and play; I'll be right here at this table," I said eyeing the snack bar.

The look I got said more than a thousand words. "I'm not allowed to go in by myself. I could get lost in there forever, Pa. Mom says I'm too precious to be lost in there forever."

"I was only kidding you, buddy," I quickly replied, trying to save face. "I wouldn't let you go anyplace where you might get lost."

Finally, having removed my jacket and shoes, I was ready to go.

Nanna and Amy had already moved into the ball area. The ball pen was a small square zone that contained hundreds of blue, red, yellow, and green plastic balls. Nanna had plunked her aching body right down in the middle of the pen, then picked up one of the plastic balls to play catch with Amy. But before she had a chance to toss it, she was bowled over by a youngster, who was far too old and too big for this little-people zone. He came flying out of the sliding tube that emptied into the ball pen and barrelled into poor, sick, unsuspecting Nanna.

Nanna disappeared in an explosion of coloured plastic balls, arms, and legs. There was a wild bout of flailing and thrashing in the ball cage before Nanna's head finally emerged from the thousands of balls. The look on her face was one of shock and disbelief as she floundered around. She was trying desperately to sit up and regain her bearings. Suddenly a second youngster, bigger than the first, flew out of the chute and crashed into Nanna just as it appeared as if she was about to regain her balance. Once more Nanna disappeared under a sea of coloured balls.

When Nanna surfaced for the second time, she wasn't waiting around for a third jolt; she was scrambling like crazy to escape. But the round balls—they refused to co-operate and stay in one place. Her every movement was foiled as balls rolled or popped away from underneath her. There was no solid place to put a hand, an arm, a hand, a foot or a leg. There was only round balls and they were making life very difficult for Nanna.

It was Amy who appeared to retaliate. She was sitting off to one side of the zone, picking up balls and throwing them at the two buffoons, the laughing hyenas, who had invaded the kiddies' play area. Nanna, looking much worse for the wear and tear, not to mention the scare she had just received, finally succeeded in scrambling out of the way. Her eyes reminded me of a cornered animal as they darted around, looking for a safe area. She finally selected what she hoped was the safest corner in the pen and crawled in. She sat with her back to the mesh wall and never took her eyes off the sliding tube.

Nanna had forgotten about playing catch, giving her undivided attention to the slide tube. It seemed that there was no end to the number of oversized youngsters who burst out of that tube. As each one hit the balls, Nanna flinched, but not Amy—she was busy picking up balls and tossing them. One at each person who plowed into the balls piled high on the bottom of the pen. Amy was laughing and giggling, throwing balls at every kid who flew out of the slide. She was protecting her Nanna.

"It makes you wonder where these maniacs' parents are, doesn't it?" I said to Nanna as I looked around the building. "Of course, there they are, in the snack bar having a coffee. Where else would they be while their children are creating havoc for everyone else?"

"C'mon, Pa, follow me!" Megan yelled. She had obviously got tired of waiting for me, and she took off into the maze known as the Discovery Zone.

She was no stranger to the Discovery Zone, as I quickly found out. She knew her way around and, like an eel, slipped with ease into and through a maze of hanging dummies. After seeing what had happened to Nanna in the kiddies ball zone, I knew that Megan needed protection, and I charged into the dummies after her.

As soon as I entered the maze of hanging dummies, I realized that Megan was the appropriate height and width—she slipped right through the maze with no trouble. I tried my best to keep up with her, but just past the first dummy in the maze some little urchin slammed a dummy in front of me, blocking my way, while another kid clipped me on the back of the knee, sending me down. I would have fallen face-first on the floor, down for the count, but the dummies prevented that. I fought my way through as best I could, crawling most of the way.

I was just crawling out of the dummies ready to say uncle when I spotted Megan racing down a corridor. She never looked back as she charged up about a dozen steps and darted into a tunnel. I was far too big to run or walk, so I crawled along behind as fast as I could, right to the head of the roller slide. I arrived just in time to hear Megan calling, urging me on.

"Follow me, Pa!" she yelled happily as she gingerly slipped through the opening at the end of the tunnel and rolled away down the slide.

I had to pause to catch my breath and assess this latest obstacle. The roller slide looked suspiciously like the kind I had used to unload trucks in another life. It was wider, but it certainly resembled an assembly-line roller slide, meant for moving large quantities of boxes or other goods in a very short time.

"I'm coming, Megan!" I called after her as she nimbly jumped off the rollers at the bottom of the slide.

But I was having a wee bit more difficulty getting out of the end of the tunnel. Head-first would have been easy; however, being somewhat of a coward, I preferred to go down slides feet-first. I struggled to get my feet, or at least my right foot, through the opening and out in front of me. This was not a simple task for a person of my size with limited sliding abilities. Somewhere behind me, crammed in the tunnel, my left leg was cramping, and my foot and knee were wedged into the walls of the tunnel. I was rapidly discovering that I had lost much of my agility and flexibility in the last fifty-eight years.

"Hurry up, Mister, you're blocking the tunnel!" some little monster yelled behind me and began to push on my derrière.

"Hold it, kid," I snarled. "I'm doing my best here."

I was struggling frantically to spring myself free so that I could catch up to Megan and protect her from the maniacs that were running loose in here while their parents were having coffee and chatting it up at the snack bar. It didn't take a brain surgeon to know that this was a place where a little girl could get seriously hurt or lost forever.

Finally I got my right foot to move and forced it out of the tunnel. I got a real good feel of the rollers — slippery, menacing, unforgiving. My left leg was reluctantly hanging onto the sides of the tunnel, and I could feel the rollers, calling, enticing me on, luring me forward. Suddenly, with a lot of help from the little maniac behind me, my left leg was forced through the tunnel, and before I could get squared around I was being propelled down the roller slide, sideways. I felt a searing pain on one cheek of my rump just before I reached the bottom, where I was unceremoniously deposited in a heap on the mat.

"It's much safer back here," said a kindly lady who was watching her child while sitting on a seat behind the barrier. She gave me a condescending smile.

"Hurry up, Pa, let's go again!" Megan hollered from the entrance to the maze, and before I could stop her, she slipped in amongst the hanging dummies. Once more I raced in after her, remembering her mothers words:

"She's much too precious to be lost forever."

Right, I thought, as I bent over to crawl through the tunnel. In front of me I got a fleeting glance of blonde hair as Megan raced ahead. Without a word she slipped through the opening and was gone down the roller slide.

Remembering the pain I had suffered on my first trip down that roller slide, I struggled to get my left foot out in front so I could turn the other cheek. I didn't have much more luck this time, as the legs and body were just as stiff trying a reverse exit. Once more the rollers picked me up and whisked me away. The rollers showed absolutely no preference for cheeks, tearing the skin from the other side just as easily as they had the first time down.

I conceded defeat. "That's it. No more roller slide," I called to Megan, who was about to enter the maze for the third time. "Let's go find Nanna and just sit for awhile."

I soon discovered that walking around to the kiddies' area was more painful than the slide had been. It seems that the two patches of missing skin were directly opposite each other, and they rubbed unmercifully with every step.

For the rest of the day at the Discovery Zone, I was doomed to sit in the section that was fenced off and full of little round plastic balls, where I couldn't get hurt. Amy and I sat side by side, throwing balls at the oafs who came flying out of the kiddies' chute. Meanwhile, Nanna took over the job of frantically chasing after Megan as she disappeared into the maze.

Megan and Amy both had a great afternoon at the Discovery Zone.

"Wasn't that great, Pa?" Megan said as I drove out of the parking lot, and I could feel the excitement in her voice. She was so pleased with her day at the Discovery Zone.

"It sure was, buddy. That was a good idea you had, to go to the Discovery Zone."

"You don't feel like you're going crazy anymore, do you, Pa?" she asked.

"No buddy, I don't feel like I'm going crazy anymore," I said.

I was pretty sure I didn't have the energy left to go crazy. I had used it all ensuring the safety of my granddaughter, even though, in hindsight, she had stood her own ground far better than I had. She was so small and agile, no one could catch her. Perhaps the next time, she could save me from the hooligans running wild at the Discovery Zone.

THE AIRPLANE RIDE

"What a great idea, a Mexican New Year!" I said when Nanna laid out her plans for New Year's. "I can't wait to see the look on Megan and Amy's faces when they get on the plane. It will be their first airplane ride."

"I'm dying to take them to the beach," Nanna said.

"You'll have to watch them like a hawk," I said and chuckled. "They're not swimming yet, you know."

"That's your job," Nanna replied. "I don't swim that well either."

"Now, don't take this wrong, Nanna, because I don't want to throw cold water on your plans, but there is one downside to taking little kids to Mexico," I said.

"What's that?" Nanna asked, almost snapping at me.

"Montezuma's revenge! What are you going to do if one of them gets sick?" I asked. After all, I thought, going to Mexico and Montezuma's revenge are two terms that are really interchangeable. Going to Mexico and getting sick seem to go hand in hand.

"Well, don't worry about that. They won't get sick," Nanna said, pooh-poohing the thought.

As the great day drew closer, the little ones — Megan, Amy, and Nanna — were wildly excited about their Mexican holiday. In their imagination and unbridled enthusiasm, they were playing on the beach and swimming in the warm waters of the Pacific Ocean long before we left Edmonton. It was amusing, for I don't believe that it ever occurred to them that not a one of them could swim.

Megan's imagination was incredible, and she could describe to me in great detail the sand castles that she was going to build on the beach. She was so excited that not even a bout of the flu, which she mysteriously contracted a week before our departure, could dampen her spirits.

"You better take Megan to the Doctor," I said to Kelly when I saw those sick little eyes.

"Don't worry, Dad," Kelly said, "the flu will run its course, and she'll be all right by the time we leave." But I had learned over the years not to take others' words literally, and I did worry.

Unfortunately, a couple of days before we were to leave, Megan was still sick. The flu had not run its course.

"I told you, you should take that child to the doctor," I grumbled to Kelly when I learned that Megan not only had a *touch* of the flu, but now was

67

experiencing a *touch* of diarrhea, and she was also throwing up. "I don't think that she should be getting on any airplane in her condition. I'm sure that we can get a doctor's certificate and get our money back," I added, but I made the mistake of talking in front of Megan.

"I'm okay! I'm okay! I don't want to go to the doctor!" Megan said as soon as the word *doctor* escaped from my lips. Somewhere in the four-and-a-half years of her short life, she had developed a terrible dislike for doctors. Even the suggestion of having to visit a doctor was enough to throw her into a tizzy.

"I don't wanna go to the doctor! I wanna go to Mexico with Nanna," she wailed.

"She's okay, Dad. I took her to the doctor yesterday," Kelly informed me in no uncertain way. The tone of her voice and the fire in her eyes told me that she was none too happy with my constant nagging. She had taken the necessary precautions, and she was capable of raising her own child.

"Oh, you did! And what did he say about taking a child in her condition on an airplane?" I asked. I was certain that any doctor worth his salt would advise against travel for this very sick little girl.

"He said she was okay. There was nothing wrong with her. It was just a slight touch of the flu and that she would be better in a couple of days. I told you, there's nothing to worry about," Kelly replied.

"Did he check her ears?" I asked. "You know, she shouldn't be flying if she has an ear infection."

"Yes, Dad, he checked her ears. He said she has a slight case of the flu, and he said she was fine."

"Did you tell him that we're taking her to Mexico?" I asked.

"Yes, I told him we were going to Mexico," came the strained response.

"Well, I'd certainly get a second opinion," I stated. "After all, doctors are only human. They make mistakes too. In fact, that's why they say they practise medicine — they're not always right, you know."

Finally, the great morning arrived. The great *early* morning that is — three o'clock came all too early. The two little sleeping beauties were dragged out of their beds and deposited into their car seats in the minivan, a mobile deep-freeze in the cold, bitter minus thirty-one degrees Celsius of a Canadian winter.

"How's Megan?" I asked as I looked into the face of a cold, freezing, shivering — albeit very excited — little girl. In her eyes I saw what only a worrywart of an old grandfather could see: sickness. There was sickness in those little eyes.

"She's fine, Dad," Kelly advised me. "We're concerned too, you know. And just for you, we did take her to emergency last night and had her checked out again. And yes, we did get a second opinion. They checked her over, even her ears, Dad — and the doctor said there was nothing wrong with her. She only has a touch of the flu. She'll be fine."

At the airport, checking in was a breeze. The check-in personnel were very pleasant and very helpful. Megan and Amy were the centre of attention. And, for the first time in my life, I enjoyed the luxury of pre-boarding.

"Sir, would you carry the baby," the gate attendant said to Bill, and pointed at Amy as we were about to leave the boarding area.

The baby, however, had her own thoughts on pre-boarding. At almost two years of age, she was very independent, and she did not like anybody to carry her. She was capable of walking all by herself, and she let everybody know it.

"Self!" she shrieked when her father reached down to pick her up. She arched her little back and kicked furiously until he put her down. "Walk-self," she snorted indignantly.

And walk she did. All the way from the attendant at the gate to her seat on the airplane she walked, all by her Self. However, by the time we reached the doors, the rest of the plane was no longer in the pre-boarding mode. The remainder of the passengers had been released. Amy led the way down the boarding ramp as speedily as a two-year-old, who stopped to inspect everything along the way, can walk, followed by a horde of passengers destined to be seated at the back of the plane.

Fortunately for those who walked behind us onto the plane, Nanna was a seasoned traveller, quite efficient in making our arrangements. We were located in the first two rows at the very front of the plane. As quickly as we entered the plane, we zipped right into our seats and the horde surged past.

"These seats are ideal," I said to Nanna. "Good job! You did very well."

Kelly, Bill, and Amy had two seats in the first row; Amy, not yet two, travelled free but didn't get her own seat; she was meant to travel on a lap. Megan, Nanna, and I were in three seats in the second row, immediately behind Kelly and Bill. Our little family was a neat, compact unit. Except for Amy, we were all strapped in our seats. Amy was bouncing around like a rubber ball, busily checking out everything about the plane. Poor Megan, on the other hand, was pale as a ghost. Her eyes looked sick; they were sunken, surrounded by big black circles. Megan was sick, and it was as if Amy was drawing all of Megan's energy.

"Someone will have to hold the baby for take off and landing," the attendant (who did not appear to like either the early shift or little kids) informed Bill as the plane was pushed away from the loading dock.

"Is no one using this seat?" Kelly asked the attendant and pointed to the vacant window seat beside her.

"Obviously not," came the attendant's curt reply.

"We'll just put Amy in this seat. Then she won't have to be held," Kelly said.

"Well," snorted the attendant, "she can sit in that seat after the plane is in the air and the Fasten Seatbelt sign has been turned off. But she's too small for a seat. Someone will have to hold her in the approved position for both takeoff and landing."

"Really? And what is the approved position?" Kelly asked.

71

"Whoever holds the baby has to use both hands, like this," she said and wrapped her arms across her chest. "Her head has to be held firmly with her face held tight to the chest."

"Good luck, Bill," Kelly chuckled.

Nanna and I smiled and leaned forward. This was one part of the trip that none of us wanted to miss. We all knew what was coming. We all chuckled (well, some of us may have laughed); all of us, that is, except Bill—he knew that he had his work cut out for him.

Now, there is another thing that Amy resented. That is to be called a *baby*, and this was the second time she had been so insulted. Since boarding the aircraft, she had been having a great time climbing about on the seats. She had checked out the first row, with Mommy and Daddy. She had checked out the second row, with Nanna, Megan, and Pa. She liked all the seats, including the vacant one that would be hers for the whole trip except takeoffs and landings. She had stopped climbing and investigating long enough to listen to the attendant's instructions, but at the sound of the word baby, her mood changed. She was not about to take the double insult. She set her jaw. Her brows furrowed. Her blue eyes darkened as she glared at the attendant.

Then Bill reached for Amy, and the rodeo was on.

Amy had been on a roll. She had energy to spare, and she was not about to lose any of it by being held down. Amy was not going to lose her high. She opened her mouth and she howled. She kicked like a mule and she squirmed like a snake. Yes, she fought like a wildcat. Bill was taking a beating as the rest of us sat back. We smiled and chuckled as we embarked on the first leg of our holiday.

Amy howled unmercifully as Bill clutched her to his chest and tried to hold her head in his hand. After all, it was the "approved method". There was no let-up as the big bird roared down the runway and rose into the early-morning skies. It was a smooth takeoff—for everyone but Bill, who looked as if he had just run the gauntlet and had been thoroughly pummeled.

"Are we having fun yet?" I asked loud enough for everyone to hear.

"I'm having fun," Kelly replied, laughing. "How are you doing, Bill?"

Bill released Amy from the "approved method" and declined to comment.

Amy never missed a beat. The second she was free she began checking out all seats again, pausing only briefly in the vacant seat next to Kelly.

Poor Megan, she sat in her seat by the window as quiet as a mouse. She didn't even object when Amy checked out her seat while she was still in it. It looked to me as if Megan was going to be sick at any minute.

"Kelly, I think Megan's going to be sick," I said as the plane reached cruising altitude.

Kelly came up out of her seat and stared at Megan, who was sitting between Nanna and me. Then she gave me that oh-no-not-again look.

"She's fine, Dad."

"She doesn't look fine to me," I replied.

Then, our meals arrived and we were in for another surprize.

73

"Excuse me," Kelly said when everyone in the plane except Amy had received a meal. "You forgot to bring Amy her meal."

"She's a baby," came the curt reply. "She didn't pay for her seat, so she doesn't get a meal."

"Are there any meals left over?" Kelly asked.

"Yes, there are, but if you haven't bought a ticket, you're not entitled to a meal."

"Well, no one told us that she wouldn't be getting a meal," Kelly said.

"You'll have to take that up with your travel agent," stated the attendant. "It's the airlines policy that you don't get a meal if you don't buy a ticket."

And so at thirty three thousand feet we began to make Amy a breakfast with a little bit from each of our plates.

When I fly, I prefer to have the seat next to the window. I find it very enjoyable and relaxing, and it makes the flight pass much more quickly. On a clear day, I enjoy the sight of the earth passing beneath the plane; I love to be able to identify the geographical features as they come into view, marking our progress. When this plane left the ground, I had had a window seat, but that quickly changed. For the first time in all my years of flying, I was involved in a game of musical chairs; Nanna was the facilitator. Everyone was shifted around, in order to get the best seat or to be next to the preferred person, who ever that might be at the moment. Not even Megan, poor little sick Megan, escaped.

I do not know how it happened, or when, but at

some point very early on in the flight, right after breakfast and the cabin had been cleaned up, Kelly, Bill, and Nanna ended up sitting in the three seats in the first row. I was in the middle seat in the second row, with Amy—the two-year-old who did not like to be held, hugged, or cuddled—snuggled up and sound asleep in my arms. Megan had laid claim to my preferred window seat and was colouring a picture. All was quiet and peaceful. I was half-asleep, settled in for a nice, relaxing flight.

Suddenly, close by and to my left, I heard an odd noise. Instantly I was awake. Very slowly, for fear of waking Amy, I turned and looked at Megan. Her face was ashen, as pale as a ghost's, and that odd noise was coming from her throat, as well as—heaven help us—from her stomach. Then, to my horror, she retched. Her whole body seemed to convulse as she fought to keep her breakfast down. She looked at me with her sick little eyes. She didn't say a word. Then she retched again, still bravely struggling to retain her breakfast.

"Kelly," I said softly, so as not to wake Amy. "I think Megan is going to be sick."

Once more, Kelly looked back over the seat.

"Are you okay, buddy?" Kelly asked.

The whole front row turned to look over the back of their seats. They all stared at the sick little girl. Megan nodded her head bravely. She didn't say a word.

"She's okay, Dad," Kelly replied, and the three in the front seat all turned away again.

"Oh great, just lovely," I mumbled sarcastically.

75

"That's easy for you to say. After all, it's only me she's going to be sick on, and you know I get sick at the smell of vomit."

"You'll let Mom know if you're going to be sick, won't you, buddy?" Kelly asked again over her shoulder.

Megan retched again and nodded her little head once more. Still there were no words.

"Kelly, I really think this little girl needs a mothers touch. You better come and get her. She's going to be sick, I know it," I pleaded. "I think she should be up there with you."

However, nobody heeded my plea for help. Nary a soul got up to help—not Mommy, not Daddy, and not Nanna.

All of the commotion, the retching and talking, had not gone unnoticed by Amy. Suddenly, without any warning, she was wide awake. She straightened up and looked around, then turned her eyes on Megan, who retched again.

"Uurrp." The sound resonated throughout the plane. Poor Megan, she was fighting desperately to keep her breakfast down. Amy turned to look at me with those big blue eyes.

"Burp," Amy responded and promptly puked all over me.

At the same time, through the smoke-colored glass that separated the common folk from the attendants, I saw movement. I noticed the attendant turn slightly and reach for something. Then she stood up. She must have heard me talking to Kelly and was assessing the situation. But she seemed to be having a bit of difficulty seeing through the smoky glass; her face was very close to the smoky glass, and her eyes seemed to be almost crossed as she tried to focus on me. I could only thank the Lord that she was taking my situation seriously. It appeared to me that she was staring intently through the smoky glass, trying to get her eyes uncrossed so that she could look right at me. Thank you lord, I muttered, thinking she was coming to my rescue.

But, to my horror, she straightened up and faced the smoked glass with a tube of lipstick in her hand, and I realized that she was really doing her makeup. About that time I felt a warm, wet, sticky feeling as vomit slowly spread across my chest and down my arm. The distinctive foul odour of vomit invaded my nostrils, then clutched at my throat, and I gagged.

"OHH FOR LOVE OF — Kelly, call the attendant!" I yelled. "I just got barfed on, it's all over me. Now would you come help me?"

"Is Megan sick?" Kelly asked, and all three in the row ahead of me spun in their seats to have a good look.

"No, it wasn't Megan, it was Amy. She got me good," I replied. "Get one of the attendants to come and give me a hand?"

However, my plea for help fell on deaf ears. The three oafs occupying the seats ahead of me had collapsed into their seats. They had been reduced to convulsing, howling idiots, they were laughing so hard.

"Amy threw up," the two-year-old advised me and pointed to the evidence of a healthy, lumpy, curdled burp that was making its way down my shirt and sleeve.

"I know, sweetheart," I replied.

Accepting the fact that no help would be coming from my travelling companions, I reached up and pushed the button calling for the attendant. I was desperately in need of help.

I glanced at the smoke-coloured glass—I knew that help was not too far away. The attendant was still looking through the glass; actually her face was almost touching it. I watched her as she moved closer to the smoke-coloured glass and was shocked to see that she was now painting on mascara.

"Amy threw up," repeated the two-year-old and once more pointed to the mess on my shirt.

"That's right, sweetheart," I replied. "Amy threw up—about two cupfuls."

That revelation was met with a renewed round of convulsive laughter from the three dolts up front. Meanwhile, vomit was soaking into my shirt and the acrid smell was rising into my nostrils. I was gagging.

"UURRRPPP," Megan retched and kept looking at me with her big blue eyes. Man, those little eyes look sick, I thought.

"Will somebody give me a hand!" I hollered loud enough to wake the dead.

My travelling companions were useless. The three of them were laughing so hard they couldn't have stood up if they tried. Again, I looked for help elsewhere. An attendant, I needed an attendant; attendants could always be counted on to help when no one else cared.

Once more I looked towards the smoked glass, which was, after all, the logical place to seek help — or so I thought. I couldn't believe what I saw. Oh, the attendant was still there all right. She was standing up, staring at me through the smoke-colored glass; her eyes were still crossed, and it looked suspiciously as if she was not poised to come to my rescue. Once more I hit the call button, and with my free arm I waved at her, beckoning her to come to my rescue. She was ignoring me completely. Then she calmly raised a tube of lipstick, put her lips through a series of contortions before stretching them out as flat and crack-free as they would go, and then slid the tube first one way across the upper lip, then the other way across the lower lip.

"What is going on?" I moaned. "Here I am, covered in puke, and the hired help stops to put on lipstick."

I knew she had to be able to see me. I could see her, even through the smoked glass, which seemed to give her a well-tanned look. I raised my dry arm and began to wave frantically.

"Excuse me!" I roared. I had to get her attention, to alert her to my plight.

Oblivious to the shouts and the flailing arm in front of her, she very calmly finished running the tube over both lips. Then put her now-rosy-red lips through another series of moves, grinding the lipstick into place. To add insult to injury she puckered her lips as if she was throwing me a kiss. Smiling contentedly she put her lipstick away.

"This is unbelievable," I moaned.

"Amy, throwed up," Amy repeated and once more

79

pointed to the mess that had seeped down the front of my shirt to my belt.

"Can you believe this?" I called to the three laughing hyenas sitting ahead of me.

I guess they could, because my comment was greeted with another round of hysterical laughter.

"Well," I mumbled, "I guess lipstick should be on straight if you're going to help a passenger who has just had one child throw up a makeshift breakfast on him while the second child is threatening more of the same from the eastern front."

I looked up once more to the attendant, hoping she had finished.

"Hey!" I yelled when, to my surprise and horror, the attendant then picked up a pair of tweezers and, right in front of me, begun to pluck her eyebrows.

By this time I had attracted the attention of everyone around me and halfway down the plane; that is, everyone around me except the attendant—this lady, *this high-flying waitress,* who obviously had no intention of responding to my arm signals or my calls for help. I'm certain that the rest of my party would have been glad to help, and had it not been for their collective fit of hysterical laughter, that left them completely immobile, they would have. For it is very difficult to kill oneself laughing and render aid to someone in need at the same time.

"Hey, attendant. You with the lipstick and the tweezers, I need some help here!" I yelled again, just in case she hadn't heard my first plea. "I need a damp cloth or something."

But she was oblivious to everything except her makeup. Through the tinted glass, I could see that she had returned to her lips. There must have been a little smear or some other imperfection, for she worked very carefully running one finger along the edge of the lower lip. I could only guess that smudges could occur if one hadn't performed the lip stretching exercises properly.

Finally Kelly was able to drag herself out of her chair and, still unable to control her fit of laughter, stagger the few steps to the front of the plane, where the attendant was still preening for all to see.

"Could we get some help back here?" I heard Kelly ask in a friendly way. Far friendlier then mine would have been at that moment; but then, she wasn't the one who had just been puked on and was facing a second attack on the left flank.

Kelly's request was met with one of the coldest stares I had ever seen. Obviously Kelly had committed the unpardonable sin — interrupting the attendant in her private world.

Kelly charged into the galley and finally returned with a handful of napkins. She was followed closely by the attendant, who diligently watched over the entire clean-up — ensuring, I assume, that everything was done according to the rules of flight.

As soon as the mop-up was complete, Kelly returned to her seat, and more laughter could be heard from the three seats ahead of me. The attendant, returned to her place, standing at the front of the aircraft behind the smoked-glass window and prepared herself to resume her duties in the cabin. She carefully brushed off her uniform with her hands. Then she tugged at the jacket and sleeves, making sure she was presentable before taking a stroll down the aisle.

Those of us seated in row 2, seats A, B, and C, went through another round of seat selection. Megan ended up in the aisle seat. I returned to my favourite seat by the window. Amy stayed only long enough in the centre seat to declare that "Something stinks!" before she left me and joined the howling trio.

Amy was right. Something did stink, me. The smell of vomit was overpowering, and once more I retched.

At that point, the attendant came out from behind the smoke glass shield, looking every bit as though she had just walked out of a beauty parlour. Every hair was in place as she began her walk through the cabin. At row 2, she suddenly stopped. She looked around and sniffed the air.

"It smells like — like vomit, like someone was sick," she said, and then shrugged her shoulders and nonchalantly strolled past.

And she was right too. It did smell like vomit and it continued to smell like vomit all the way to Mexico. As we departed from the plane, the warm humid air hit me like a blast furnace and the smell of vomit grew stronger. Again I gagged.

It was the quickest I was ever checked through customs in Mexico. When I arrived at the door where you push the button hoping for a green light, the nice señorita took one whiff and waved me right through. Even the taxi driver cursed his misfortune at having us as his fare. He reached our hotel in record time even by Mexican standards.

The trip had been an exhausting, stinking ordeal. It was twelve hours since we had rustled the kids out of bed. They were tired, and we all collapsed onto the couches in the hotel lobby as Nanna went to check us in. I noticed that all my travelling companions chose a couch a healthy distance away from me.

"You're not going to believe this!" Nanna declared when she returned.

"I believe it," I replied, "but can't it wait until we get into our room? I really do want a shower."

"Well, your shower will just have to wait!" she said. "They just told me that they don't have a reservation for us, and they're full up. There's no room at the inn!"

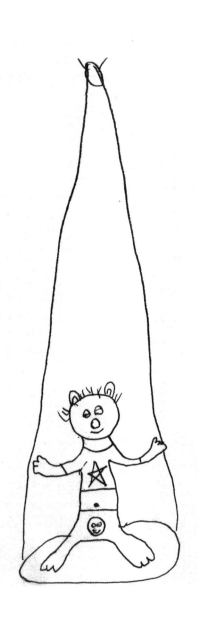

PA'S TREAT

"Don't worry, I'll look after the girls. They'll be just fine. In fact, I think that I might just take them out for supper," I said to Kelly, offering my services as a babysitter, and at the same time assuring her that her children, my granddaughters Megan and Amy, were in good hands. Yes, eating was always high on my list of priorities; and going out to eat good food was one of the great pleasures in life. I loved eating good food, and sharing that experience with the girls only made it better.

Since Kelly and I had published our first book, *The Stump Farm*, this was a scenario that would often be repeated. Mar was still working full-time. Kelly and Bill were both teaching full-time. I was retired. And on top of this busy schedule, we were all active with our new

85

book-selling adventure. Everyone was committed, and everyone—with the exception of the happily retired "old guy"—was double- or triple-booked. On this night I would be the first one home, and available to relieve the babysitter and spend some quality time with the girls.

"Oh, that would be nice," Kelly replied. "They'll like that."

"Good," I said, "consider it done. Oh, by the way, do you have any idea where they might like to go?"

"They'll change their minds four hundred times between now and then," she laughed. "But just ask them, Dad. They'll tell you what they want. Oh, and good luck."

"How about you giving me just a wee bit of a hint—you know, like which was their favourite restaurant today, or even yesterday?" I asked. I always found it easier for me and more enjoyable for them if I had a little knowledge of what my granddaughters liked the last time out. It seemed to give me a little bit of an edge.

"Just ask them, Dad," Kelly repeated. She sounded a little tired and worn. "They have minds of their own; they'll tell you what they like."

*   *   *   *   *

I bounced out of bed at five-thirty in the morning. By nine I had finished a live radio interview, as well as a newspaper interview. Then I drove for two hours to a book-signing that Kelly had set up for me at least a month earlier. Arriving at the appointed time, I found out that the staff in the bookstore were not quite ready for me (actually, they admitted later that they had forgotten I was coming). I set up my own display, signed more than one hundred books, and I talked to several hundred people. I was hungry when I took down my display and loaded it into my car. I fought the urge to stop and feed my growling belly.

As I drove the two hours to pick up my granddaughters, one lesson was quickly becoming apparent: I was not as young as I used to be. It had been a long, long day, and I was just a wee mite tired and a whole lot hungrier when I pulled up in front of Kelly's house at five-thirty in the afternoon to pick up Megan and Amy. When my grandchildren raced to the door to greet me, though, I couldn't hide the smile that crossed my face, for I no longer felt tired. Oh, I was still hungry, but there was one thing I knew for sure—my day was just about to get a whole lot better.

Amy, the three-year-old, was the first one to meet me at the door. She was just bouncing off the wall, as excited as I had ever seen her. My first thought was that, in preparation for Pa, the babysitter had fed her a big bag of candy.

"Hi, Amy, how's Pa's girl?" I asked, greeting her as I walked into the house. She ignored the question, and turned and raced away.

"Megan! Megan!" Amy yelled excitedly. "Pa's here. Pa's here now. C'mon Pa, you can watch our dress-up."

It was a greeting that warmed the heart, the sort that I would never get tired of. Not only had the fatigue that had dogged me for the last one hundred kilometers vanished, but for the moment the hunger pangs just melted away. Suddenly I felt young and alive.

"Hi, Pa," Megan greeted me as she came bounding down the stairs.

"Hi, buddy," I replied. "How's my girl?"

"I'm fine, Pa," she replied.

"Are you girls all ready to go for supper?" I asked.

87

"I hope you're hungry, because Pa's hungry enough to eat a horse."

"Really?" Megan said, staring at me like she couldn't believe what she had just heard. Her eyes were wide open at the thought of someone eating a horse.

"It's just a saying, buddy," I said. "Pa doesn't really eat horses."

"Oh, okay," she replied, but the look in her eye said that at that moment she didn't really believe me.

"Pa, can you watch our dress-up?" Amy asked once more, ignoring my question.

"They've been practicing their dress-up all afternoon, said Ellie, the babysitter informing me of the pre-arranged plan as she prepared to walk out the door. "They've been excited waiting for you to get here so they could show you their dress-up play."

"I can believe that," I said. "I know they love to play dress-up."

"Can you, Pa?" asked Amy again, and she was just bouncing. "Can you watch us play dress-up?"

"I sure can, buddy," I replied. "But first, I would suggest that we go out for supper."

"But then can we play dress-up?" Amy asked.

"Then you can play dress-up." I smiled.

"Okay," Amy said happily. "Megan, Pa said we can play dress-up after we eat," she added for her sister's benefit.

"Who's going to pay for supper?" I asked.

Both little girls stopped and gave me a questioning look.

"You, Pa," said Megan gravely. "We don't have any money."

"Me?" I asked, feigning a look of surprise.

"Yeah, we don't gots no money, Pa," added Amy,

and her voice was very serious.

"Okay, then it's Pa's treat," I said and laughed. "Where would you girls like to go tonight?"

"It doesn't matter," Megan said and shrugged her little shoulders.

"We could play dress-up, Pa," Amy said.

"Yes, we could, but we're going to play dress-up after supper. Let me think now," I said. "Since it's Pa's treat . . . I say we can go wherever you want. How does that sound?"

"But-but where do we want to go?" Megan asked, and she too was very serious.

"Hmm. Well, I guess we could go to—" I started to say.

"I know," Megan suddenly chimed in excitedly, "let's go to Boston Pizza."

Hmm, Boston Pizza. Not really my favourite, I thought, but not altogether a bad choice; after all, I do really like their Thai Chicken salad. And once more my stomach began to growl, anticipating the tangy meal.

"I want to go to Bing's," Amy piped up.

Well now, a good feed of Chinese food was a very good suggestion too. Once more my imagination kicked in, and I could not only picture an appetizer of dry ribs and a heaping dish of Special Chow Mein, but I could actually smell them. My mouth was watering.

"But, Amy, we had Bings last night," Megan objected.

"We had Bing's bring-in," Amy said. "We didn't go out to Bings."

"I want to go to Boston Pizza," Megan countered.

"But, Megan," Amy said very seriously, and her little eyes grew wide with excitement, "Bing's got spring rolls."

89

"I don't want spring rolls," Megan answered. "I want Dino Fingers."

"Okay, girls," I interjected. "Pa's got to make one phone call. I want you two to decide which place we're going to go to for supper. Can you do that?" They both looked at me; neither said a word. "I'll go downstairs and make the call. Remember, you two have to agree on where we're going. Okay?"

Not a word, only silence, and they both watched me as I left the room.

When the call was finished, I came back upstairs.

"Okay, girls, have we decided yet?" I asked.

They were both standing in the same spots where I had left them. Neither one was talking. They both watched me walk back into the room and continued to look at me.

"Pa's hungry, girls, so where are we going — to Boston Pizza or Bing's?" I asked. They both stood there for the longest time, looking at me expectantly with their big eyes wide open. Finally it was Megan who spoke.

"I want to go to Boston Pizza," she said.

"How about you, Amy, how does Boston Pizza sound for tonight? We can go to Bing's next time, I promise," I said.

Instantly the expectant look on Amy's innocent little face changed to the most disappointed scowl I had ever seen. Her eyebrows dropped like heavy, dark storm clouds. Her little face puckered up and the bottom lip popped way out. She never said a word, just stood there, glaring at me.

"You better be careful," I said, kidding her, hoping to relieve the tension, "or you'll step on that bottom lip."

But she did not smile; the storm clouds only grew heavier and more ominous. She continued to glare.

I had the feeling that Boston Pizza was not on the menu for tonight; however, I thought I would try one more time.

"Would you like to go to Boston Pizza with Pa and Megan?" I asked again.

"No!" she stated emphatically.

"Well, what would you like, then?" I asked.

"I want to know what time my dad is coming home," Amy said, changing the subject. "I want my Dad!"

Much to Amy's relief, it was Bill who was the first to walk through the door shortly after eight, while we were busy playing dress-up. She was the first to react.

"Megan! Megan! Mom and Dad are home," Amy sang out loudly as she raced to the door to greet them. "Do you want to watch us play dress-up, Dad?" She was as excited as she had been when I walked in three hours earlier.

"Hi, girls," Bill said.

"Did the girls eat supper?" Kelly asked.

"Oh yeah, you betcha!" I replied. "They both ate like little troopers."

"Yeah, it was Pa's treat tonight," Amy replied, and her eyes were wide with excitement.

"Good, and where did Pa take you for supper?" Kelly asked.

"We stayed at home," Megan said, "and Pa cooked his favourite supper."

"Yeah, I saved a couple for you," I said. "Your hot dogs are in the fridge."

"Hot dogs!" Kelly exclaimed. She burst out laughing, and the look on her face said it all.

91

Kelly was familiar with my distaste for hot dogs as a meal; in fact, when she was growing up, if ever you wanted a fight, all Martha had to cook was hot dogs and the battle was on.

"Pa, don't tell me that you stayed home and that you had . . . hotdogs?"

"Yeah. We stayed home and Pa maked us hot dogs," Amy warbled happily.

"But Pa, you don't like hotdogs," Kelly said, enjoying the moment and reminding me that I never did consider hot dogs a meal.

"Yes he does," Amy quickly chimed in, defending me. "Pa likes hot dogs. You said you like hot dogs, didn't you, Pa?"

"Pa ate four hot dogs for supper," Megan said, and she had the cutest little smile as she confirmed Amy's report.

"What can I say?" I said and smiled at my granddaughters. "We had several choices, and tonight, hot dogs were our favourite food."

PATCHY

The relationship that develops between children and their pets is a wondrous thing. It is a bond that is everlasting. Sometimes children share relationships with their grandparents, and the relationship becomes sort of a triangle. Nanna and I have been very fortunate, because we have this type of relationship with our grandchildren and their pets. It could be said that I was doubly blessed — very fortunate because as a youngster I experienced a similar relationship with my grandfather and my pets.

I am always amazed by little incidents in our lives that knot the ties that bind, and cement the bonds ever deeper. The bonds between Megan and Amy, their puppies, and Nanna and Pa are firmly cemented. One incident that comes to mind involved my granddaughter Amy and her puppy Patchy, a red miniature poodle she absolutely adores. The incident occurred during the wee hours of the morning at a time when we had guests. Not just any guests, but very special guests, for both Megan and Amy were having a sleepover at Nanna and Pa's house. A sleepover was always much more fun if it was a pretend camp-out. And Nanna was the best pretend camper ever. She could make a pretend camp out of anything.

The camp, as always, was pitched on the floor right beside Nanna and Pa's bed. The first item on the agenda was the tent. Everyone knows that a pretend camp-out could not occur without a tent. Two chairs had been placed strategically beside our bed. They were about six feet apart, facing away from each other. Then Nanna had stretched a large sheet over the chair backs of the chairs to cover the area where the bed was to go and provide the necessary shelter for the campers. For a mattress, Nanna had spread several layers of blankets and pillows over the rug, and on top of all this padding Nanna had unrolled two of Pa's eiderdown sleeping bags. One sleeping bag served as the bottom sheet; the other as both top sheet and blanket. The girls had been tucked into their camp-out beds and were sleeping like two little angels.

Of course, no sleepover would be complete unless the girls could bring their puppies with them. When I went to bed, Megan and her dog Spunky were curled up on one side of the camp, and Amy and Patchy were curled up on the other side.

Soon I was in a sound sleep, having a dream, a fitful

dream about another time in my life. It was a time when a dog was a large part of my life. I was back on the Stump Farm in the log house my father built; and the front half of Bunny, the dog that I shared with my sister Judy, was whining. The whining of the front half, Judy's half of the dog, always meant that the back half of Bunny, my half of the dog, needed immediate attention — and if she didn't get it, I was the one who had to clean up her mess. It was the whining of the dog that woke me up. The sound was distant, but still it sounded so real.

Suddenly I was wide awake and sat upright in bed. I sat there listening for sounds, but at that moment there were none. The house was quiet as a morgue, and I relaxed, thankful that it was only a dream. I breathed a sigh of relief and lay down again. I smiled to myself; it was only a false alarm.

It had been a long time since we had had dogs in the house on a permanent basis. There had been dogs on the Stump Farm that were pets of one or more of my brother and sisters. And both of our daughters had dogs for pets when they were at home; but in the later years dogs had not been a big part of our lives. It wasn't that Mar and I didn't like dogs — we did. In fact Mar, like our granddaughters, absolutely adores dogs; however, our lifestyle took us away from home so often that we decided against having one. I always figured it was unfair to the dog if a person was not home to take care of it.

I was just dozing off again when a sound cut through the air like a shrill whistle. It was a sound that

I had heard often in my life: it was the distinct sound of a dog whining. This wasn't part of any dream. It was the real thing. I suddenly remembered that we did have a couple of dogs in the house, and one or both of them was sending us a message. This was not a message for me, however; this was a message for Nanna, for it was she who always responded to the dogs in their hour of need in the early morning.

"Nanna . . . Nanna," I whispered, and I reached across the bed and gently nudged her with my foot.

"What do you want?" she muttered groggily. Her sleepy voice was weak even for a whisper.

"I don't want anything," I said, "but I believe the dogs do. I heard one of the dogs calling your name. I think they both may have to go out."

At that point the whining resumed, and it reached a feverish pitch.

"I didn't hear anything," she replied and rolled over to continue her sleep.

"What do you mean, you didn't hear anything!" I said, not believing what she had just said. "You're not deaf, so don't tell me you can't hear all that whining downstairs. Listen to that call. It's saying 'Nanna, Nanna! Let me out before I piddle on your floor."

"Well, I can't hear anything. If you hear dogs whining, then you better go and let them out before one of them does go on my rug," she said.

"I thought that was supposed to be your job," I complained as I stumbled from my bed in the darkness. Normally I would have turned a light on, but not with Megan and Amy asleep in our bedroom.

"I'm coming," I mumbled, hoping that the dogs would hear me and the girls wouldn't.

Before going downstairs to let the dogs out, I checked on the girls. I was relieved to find that the little angels were still sleeping. But sure enough, both dogs were missing.

Not wanting to be the one to awaken one of our sleeping beauties, I tippytoed quietly down stairs in the dark. Enough light was coming from the outside that I could see there was only one dog at the front door. It was Patchy, Amy's dog, who was dancing around in a friendly greeting. It was obvious to me that she had to go, by the way she was prancing around my feet on her hind legs and scratching my legs with her forepaws.

"Good girl, Patchy," I said, praising her for asking to go out. Then I unlocked the patio door, slid it open, and stepped to the side to let her out. It was there that I got the message. It was soft and warm, and it had squished up between my toes. Piddle it wasn't. Patchy hadn't been whining to get out to relieve herself—she had already done her job on the tile beside the door. As if she knew what she had done was wrong, she tucked her tail between her legs and began to slink away.

"Come here, Patchy," I called to her. "Bad dog! You go outside, now." I reached down to pick her up and put her out. In the faint light I saw her drop to her belly, to get as close to the floor as possible, and she made a dash for the other side of the room. Patchy faked a move to the right and then tried to slip between me and the railing on the left. I reacted instinctively and took a step towards the railing to head her off.

I missed Patchy, but I did not miss the second message that had been deposited on the tile. My foot slipped in doggy-doo and shot out from under me like an arrow. I lost my balance and frantically grabbed for support, I caught the railing and spun around. Somehow I kept myself from falling, but my momentum only helped to drive my big toe into one of the spindles in the railing. A sharp pain shot through my foot and up my leg. I stifled the scream that had leapt up in my throat while I struggled to stay upright. I finally regained my balance, but not before I had smeared every tile within reach with doggy-doo. Standing in the dark, I realized that I had both feet smeared with doggy-doo and a throbbing big toe that felt like it was broken.

"Patchy, get over here, right now!" I called as I hobbled over to the door and turned on the light. A quick glance told me that Patchy had had enough of me and my wild antics. She was nowhere in sight. Like a phantom, she had melted into the night. The house was deathly silent as I surveyed the mess on the floor.

One pile of doggy-doo bore the imprint of three toes in it—my three toes. The other pile was smeared across several tiles, coming to an abrupt halt at the railing.

I limped over to the cupboard, dug out a bar of soap, and then climbed onto the countertop. I put both feet into the sink and washed them. My big toe was about twice its normal size and was throbbing like crazy. When I was finished washing my feet, I got down on my hands and knees and wiped up the floor.

Then I remembered: Dogs whining in the middle of

the night and finding dog-poo in unexpected places at unexpected times were two more reasons that I didn't have a dog anymore.

"Did you let the dogs out?" asked Nanna as I carefully limped into the darkened bedroom.

Nanna, who couldn't hear the dogs whining a few minutes earlier had miraculously regained her hearing. She heard me as I limped into the bedroom on a carpeted floor. Now she seemed to be very much awake.

"Oh yeah," I replied, and I waited for my eyes to adjust to the dark so I could check on the girls and see if I could find where Patchy had disappeared to.

"Did you watch them to make sure they went to the bathroom?" Nanna asked.

"Oh, they went to the bathroom all right," I said. "I can swear to that."

"Where's Amy?" I asked when I crept over to the tent to check on the girls. I was startled to see that there was only one girl, Megan, and one dog, Spunky, in the camp.

"Nanna, where's Amy?" I asked again.

But Nanna was once again sound asleep; she didn't here me. I searched around the camp. Then I checked the spare bedroom. Finally I came back to our bedroom and turned on the light. There in my bed, on my side of the bed, was Amy, and like an angel she was also sound asleep. Curled up beside her as close as she could get, with her tail wagging a mile a minute and giving me that big brown eyed, I'm happy to see you look, was her doggy, Patch.

"What is the matter with you? Turn out that light," Nanna, who was suddenly wide awake again, scolded me. "You're going to wake the girls."

Obediently I turned out the light. I limped over to the closet and grabbed a blanket, and then gingerly, very gingerly, I made my way downstairs. I sat down on the chesterfield and slowly hoisted my foot up onto the arm to try to relieve the throbbing in my toe; then I leaned back and closed my eyes. At least I was now better placed, I thought, just in case the puppies needed me, or one of the girls needed a glass of milk.

I could not help but smile. This wasn't the old Bob Adams, I chuckled. In my younger days, it was I who would be sleeping in my bed, and the puppy would have spent the rest of the night outside.

I closed my eyes and drifted off to sleep. And that night, I dreamed of a little girl and her dog sleeping comfortably in her grandfather's bed.

THE PLAYGROUND

I'm never going to survive being a grandfather, I thought as I leapt over the teeter-totter and barrelled around the end of the swings, dodging two youngsters on the swings who were reaching for the stars. My goal was to get to the monkey bars as fast as I could and save the life of my granddaughter Megan.

Megan had been on the swings and I had taken my eyes off her for only a second when Amy called. "Watch me, Pa! Watch me!"

And watch her I did, with my heart in my throat, as she scampered up the spiralling steps before falling backwards and sliding headfirst down the spiralling slide. I raced for the bottom of the slide to try and catch her before she flew off the end and cracked her little head on the ground. Before I could reach her, she spread her arms and legs, forcing her shoes and hands against the sides of the slide. Her timing was perfect, and she skidded to a stop right at the bottom of the slide. Then, as calmly as can be, she flipped over and jumped to the ground.

"Did you see me, Pa?" Amy asked excitedly. "Did you see me?"

"Yes, I certainly did," I moaned, "and I just about had a heart attack. Now, I hope I never see you do that again. That's a good way to get hurt—and you don't want to get hurt, do you?"

"I won't get hurt, Pa," Amy assured me. "Daddy lets me slide down the slide like this all the time."

"He does?" I blurted out. "That's unbelievable!" What father in his right mind would let my granddaughter pull a suicidal stunt like that, I thought. "I'm sure your daddy doesn't want to see you get hurt," I said.

"My daddy says I can go down the slide backwards if I want to!" Amy stated emphatically.

Then I took a glance back over my shoulder to where Megan had been—over on the swings, playing with a couple of other kids, whose parents or grandparents were nowhere to be seen. But she was not at the swings now. Oh, the other two kids were still there; and they were swinging back and forth, having a great time. I frantically looked around for Megan, and when I spotted her, I just about died.

"No, Megan!" I moaned.

My oldest grandchild had moved over to the monkey bars—actually, she was on the very top bar with her knees locked over the bar, and she was hanging upside down. Look Pa, no hands! My heart skipped a beat as I rapidly tried to think of the best thing I could do to save her. I knew I didn't dare call to her to warn her of the dangers; I was afraid that the sudden sound of my bellowing voice would be just enough distraction to make her lose her concentration. How would I ever explain to her mother that I was irresponsible and neglectful, and had caused the slip that was fatal . . . or at the very least bad enough to have resulted in a broken neck and—heaven forbid!—paralysis. One thing I did know: I had to get over to those monkey bars and save Megan.

I forgot about Amy and immediately charged across the playground. I raced past, dodged around, and leapt over the play-ground equipment in my haste to get to the scene of the accident before it happened. I breathed a sigh of relief when I arrived under the bars before she fell.

"Here, Megan," I said as quietly and as calmly as I could muster the words, "Pa's here, don't be afraid. I'll get you down."

But Megan had other ideas.

"I'm not afraid, Pa," she said as she calmly reached up with one hand, grabbed onto the bar, and pulled herself up. I stood below and braced myself to catch her when she fell.

"Be careful, buddy," I said in a whisper, for fear of startling her. "Oh, please be careful."

"See, Pa, I'm not afraid," Megan said as she very calmly settled herself on the top of the bar—and then let go with both hands.

"Hang on, Megan, I'll save you!" I wanted to yell, but the words froze in my throat. I could only stand there and stare helplessly up at her.

"Do you want to see me hang by my knees?" she asked in a very calm voice.

"No!" I blurted out. "I want to see you down here. Here on the ground, where it's nice and safe."

"It's safe up here, Pa," she replied. "I do this all the time."

"Yeah, well, I—I don't want you playing on the monkey bars when Pa is with you," I said.

"Why?"

"Because . . ." I said trying to think of some really good reason, but I couldn't.

"Because why, Pa?"

"Because—because it's not safe, buddy," I replied trying to maintain my appearance of calm as she sat on that bar without holding onto anything.

"Why is it not safe, Pa?"

"Because it's not, buddy. You might slip and fall and hurt yourself real bad. Now come on and I'll help you down."

"Why will I hurt myself, Pa?"

"Because when you fall from the top of the monkey bars, it's a long way down. And you can be very seriously hurt when you hit the ground."

"No, I won't," she said. "Mom lets me play on the monkey bars all the time and I don't get hurt."

"Well, buddy, Pa might get hurt."

"Why?"

"Because I don't think Pa's heart can take much more of you and Amy in the playground."

"Why?"

"Because Pa's getting too old for this kind of play," I said. "Why don't you come down, and we'll all go for an ice cream?"

"Okay, Pa," she said.

"Thank you," I said and took a deep breath. "That's a good girl."

I finally relaxed when Megan reached down and firmly grabbed the bar with both hands as she prepared for her descent. But my relief was short-lived. As quick as a wink, she flipped over backwards, and my heart just about stopped. I made a lunge for her, but she never made it that far. She slipped over the bar expertly; only her knees stopped her from plummeting to my outstretched arms and the ground. I was terrified at what was happening and afraid to move. Then she let go of the bar with her hands and was again dangling by her knees from the bar.

"See, Pa?" she said. "I'm not afraid! This is easy! I won't fall."

"Oh my Lord," I mumbled when she reached up and grabbed the bar again. Then she straightened out her legs and did a back-flip. I made a feeble attempt to catch her, but I was to slow, and she landed effortlessly, on both feet, on the ground.

"Megan, are you okay?" I asked, afraid of what the answer could be.

"Can we go for ice cream now?" she asked.

"Yes, we can," I said and breathed a sigh of relief.

Finally I felt that, with a little luck, I might just survive the day.

Then I turned around to call Amy. I was just in time to see her flop over on her back at the top of the slide and once more shoot down the spiral slide headfirst on her back.

"Oh, no!" I moaned. That's it, I thought, I've got to get away from here. Now. It didn't help my poor old shot nerves any when she slid to a halt at the bottom, flipped over and calmly skipped off the slide into the sand.

"C'mon girls. No more slides. No more monkey-bars. Let's go for an ice cream."

Over ice cream, I thought back to a few years earlier — well, maybe it was thirty years — to the days when my own children were young.

*   *   *   *   *

We were living in Hinton at the time. We had just sat down at the supper table. I had been up since five in the morning, working at my day job. After supper I would be working on the house I was building.

"What did you do today?" I asked Kelly, my oldest daughter, who was five years old.

"Me and Robin went to the playground today," she said, "an' we played on the swings and the merry-go-round!"

"Well, isn't that good," I said, thinking that when I was a kid we didn't even have playgrounds. "Did Mommy go with you, or did you go by yourselves?"

"We went all by ourselves!" Kelly replied proudly.

"Well, that was nice of you to take your little sister."

"We went on the slides, and the monkey bars too!" she said and her eyes lit up at the very thought of her day.

"Well, that's good. It sounds to me as if you both had a great day," I said as I scooped myself up a second helping of mashed potatoes and smothered them with gravy.

*   *   *   *   *

Yes, I thought, times have really changed. When I was a kid, I took my brother and sisters to the McLeod River for a day of swimming. When Kelly was only five, she was taking her little sister to the playground for the afternoon. Today, I can't bear the thought of letting my grandkids walk across the street by themselves.

What's wrong with this picture, I thought, when I can't or won't let my granddaughters go to the playground and have the same kind of fun and experience that my children enjoyed? Is this what this world is coming to? Is it city living? Or am I just getting old?

No, I thought, that's not it. Now I'm a grandfather, I'm wiser than a whole treeful of owls, and suddenly all the rules have changed.

THE GOLDFISH

"Hi, Hon, we're home," Nanna called out as she walked through the door, "and I've brought a little guest to see you."

"Hi, Pa," Amy said. Her voice did not have the usual lively ring to it.

"We've got something for you," Nanna said and her voice sounded like gloom and doom.

Something dreadful had transpired.

Amy charged ahead of Nanna. She was anxious to get to me first, which she did, and she handed me an unexpected little present. I say "little", because that is exactly what it was. A very small plastic grocery bag — the kind you would expect to find one or (if you were really lucky) two tiny candies in. The way the bag was flying around as she ran towards me, I thought for sure it was empty. Were Nanna and Amy playing a joke on me?

"Here, Pa. We brought you this," Amy said. She was puffing as if she had run all the way over to our house.

"Well, isn't that nice," I said and I gave her a hug and a big smile. "A present for Pa, what a pleasant surprise. Why, thank you Amy, that was very thoughtful of you. I know, I know," I said as I lifted the little bag "I have to guess what it is, don't I?"

Guessing what a present is has become somewhat of a tradition. It would be unthinkable to open a present without the customary stab or two at what lies hidden within. I carefully inspected the plastic grocery bag as I prepared to venture my guess. The first thing I noted was its weight: whatever was inside did not appear to weigh any more than the plastic bag itself.

At that point Amy gave me a funny little look, and then she looked at Nanna with a questioning look. Obviously Pa hadn't responded in the way he was expected to.

"Could it be something to eat?" I asked. I expected a hearty *yes* since, after all, the gift appeared to have come from a grocery store and, I presumed, directly from the store to me.

"No!" she said, and once more the funny questioning glance at Nanna.

"Well, it could be, but it's not," Nanna replied.

"Yuk," Amy groaned and gave Nanna a disgusted look.

"Well now, then, I wonder what it could be," I said, trying to put a little emotion into my voice.

Having been unsuccessful in my attempt to guess what the contents of the bag were I made a big deal of opening the plastic bag and taking a quick, sneaky peek at the interior. I got a glimpse of gold and white and what I thought could be scales on the tiny object that was sticking to the folds of plastic at the bottom of the bag. I quickly closed the bag and looked at the bearers of this strange gift.

"What is this?" I asked as I slowly reopened the bag and confirmed what I had seen with the first peek. It was gold and white all right, and it did have scales on it. "Is this some sort of a joke?"

"Well, what does it look like?" Mar replied, and her voice had a very sympathetic, grandmotherly ring to it.

"It looks like . . . like a dead goldfish," I replied.

"It is a dead goldfish, Pa," Amy replied as tears filled her eyes.

"I can see that it's a goldfish, buddy," I said sympathetically. "What am I supposed to do with it? It's dead. Isn't it?" I said to Mar, giving her a questioning look.

"My goldfish, Sunflower, died, Pa!" Amy said, and the tears that had welled up in the corners of her eyes began to roll down her cheeks.

"Oh, that's too bad, buddy," I said, and I put all the compassion I could muster into my reply as I tried to comfort her. After all, the loss of a pet — even a goldfish — is a very traumatic event when you're three years old.

Amy stood beside Nanna in front of me. Both were

113

suddenly very quiet; it was an unusual situation. However, they both stood there staring at me, expectantly. Obviously I was supposed to do something, but what?

"How did he die?" I finally asked, breaking the silence, as I gazed down upon the lifeless body of Sunflower.

"Sunflower's not a he, Pa. Sunflower's a girl," Amy informed me.

"Sorry, buddy," I replied. I should have known there are only girls in the family.

"Amy asked me if I knew why Sunflower died, and I told her I didn't know," Mar replied. "And I told her I thought we should flush her down the toilet, because that's what I always did whenever one of Kelly's goldfish died. But then Amy screamed at me, 'No! Don't flush Sunflower down the toilet. I'm going to save her and show her to Pa. Pa will know why Sunflower died. Pa knows everything!'" Nanna blurted out, mimicking Amy's outburst.

"You can tell me why Sunflower died. Can't you Pa?" Amy said, looking at me with expectant eyes. "You know everything about animals!"

"I do?" I said without thinking. For a moment I stood and I stared helplessly into an innocent pair of eyes that were looking at me with great expectation. Suddenly I was awash in a good-for-nothing, hopeless, helpless feeling that swept my body. "Oh, yes, of course I do."

"I told her that you didn't know everything, that you just think you do, but she insisted on bringing

114

Sunflower over here so that you could look at her," Mar said and shrugged her shoulders.

"Why yes, of course I know everything!" I said, not wanting to destroy the faith of a little girl. All the while I was stalling for time, trying to think of something profound to say. "Well, let me see . . .," I said as I began to fumble my way through this trying situation. "First, I think I'm going to need a napkin or a Kleenex or something like that."

"I'll get it!" Amy yelled and raced into the bathroom, returning with half a roll of toilet paper trailing behind her. "Here, Pa."

"That's perfect, buddy," I said. I tore a leaf from the roll and laid it out on the table. Then I opened the plastic bag, and with two fingers I reached down and picked up the remains of Sunflower. Holding her by the tail, I turned her around slowly and eyeballed her from every angle. Amy was right beside me, giving Sunflower a real good once-over too.

"Do you see anything that might have caused Sunflower to die?" I asked Amy.

"I can't see anything, Pa," she said.

Then I laid poor old Sunflower on the piece of toilet paper and stood back and looked at her. Amy stepped back beside me; but she wasn't looking at Sunflower, she was looking at me, expecting some words of wisdom.

"What do you think, Amy, should we check her fins and see if there's any fin rot there?" I asked, still stalling for time while I tried to think of something to tell this little girl who had so much faith in her grandfather's knowledge.

"Okay, Pa," she said, "I think we should check her fins."

Very carefully, I took a tip of each fin between my fingers and stretched them out one at a time. Amy and I both had our noses right down close to Sunflower during this part of the examination.

"Did you see any fin rot?" I asked her when the last fin dropped and returned to its normal place, plastered to the side of Sunflower.

"I don't think so, Pa," Amy replied as she took another look at the last fin. "It looks just like it always did except it's stuck to her side now."

"What about Sunflower's eyes? I think her eyes look good," I said. "How do Sunflower's eyes look to you, Amy?"

"They look good to me, Pa."

"That's what I thought," I said. "I guess we should check her gill covers, then."

"What are gill covers?" she asked.

"These are the gill covers," I replied, and I lifted the cover with a toothpick. "You see, Amy, Sunflower breathes through her gills. They're very delicate and need protection, and that is what the gill covers do. They protect the gills. Now, it appears that Sunflower's gills are okay too—see how red they are?"

"Are they supposed to be red, Pa?"

"Yes they are, buddy, and Sunflower's gills are nice and red. So that isn't the reason she died. Sunflower must have died from natural causes," I said.

"She did?" Amy asked and her eyes suddenly got real big.

"Absolutely. You see, Amy, that is just how Mother Nature planned it. Some species like goldfish are actually food for other fish and animals, and Mother Nature makes sure that species like goldfish produce hundreds and even thousands of babies. That's because most of them will die or be eaten before they get very big. You gave Sunflower a good home; you fed him—I mean, her—every day just like you were supposed to; and you gave her clean water.

"I did, Pa," Amy said very seriously.

"What about bigger fish? Were there any bigger fish in the bowl that might have tried to eat her?"

"No," she replied and shook her head. "But if a bigger fish tried to eat her, then she would be gone into the bigger fish's stomach. Wouldn't she, Pa?"

"Yes, she would have, Amy. If the bigger fish had swallowed her, she sure would have been gone, into the bigger fish's stomach."

"I don't have a bigger fish," Amy said.

"I know," I replied. "But Sunflower died anyway. Didn't she?"

"Uh-huh," she said.

"You know, buddy, you did an excellent job of feeding and taking care of Sunflower. I know that because many goldfish never even survive the trip from the pet shop to the home . . .," and I continued to talk, hoping that I could ease the pain she was obviously feeling at having lost Sunflower.

"See, Nanna, I told you Pa would know why

117

Sunflower died," Amy said, suddenly cutting me off. She was quite satisfied with my ramblings.

"Well, since Pa, knows everything, you should ask him what he wants to do with Sunflower now," Nanna said, shaking her head as if she couldn't believe what she had just heard.

"It's okay, Nanna, you can flush Sunflower down the toilet now," Amy told a somewhat startled Nanna.

"But—" Nanna started to reply. Amy cut her off.

"Do you guys have any treats?" Amy asked as she headed to the goodie cupboard, leaving Nanna and me to stare at the dead goldfish lying on the kitchen table.

THE RULE-FOLLOWERS

I love the fact that my granddaughters are rule-followers. To me, it's amazing that they only have to be advised of a rule once, and it's forever remembered. When a rule is broken, they will not only remind the perpetrator of the no-no they have just committed, they will often quote the source of the rule with great accuracy. There is a stern look on the little face and a very serious, no-nonsense tone in the voice, as the violator is advised of the error of his or her ways. These reprimands have on occasion been known to be just a wee bit of an irritation — especially to Nanna, for Nanna has been known to bend the rules on occasion. And Megan and Amy do not hesitate to scold anyone who fails to follow the rules.

One incident in particular always brings a smile to

my face whenever it comes to mind. It occurred on a beautiful warm summer afternoon. Nanna and I had the pleasure of spending this glorious day with our granddaughters—Megan, age six, and Amy—age three—without the interference of parents.

At the appointed hour we picked the girls up at their home in Spruce Grove. They were dressed appropriately, as was Nanna, in shorts and T-shirts, for an afternoon in the great outdoors. One of the girls' favourite places to go on a day like this was Dog Rump Creek Park in Stony Plain. Megan and Amy absolutely loved this little park and the amenities within. They would have a great time playing on the old train—actually the caboose—that still retained the steps and the landing leading to the door and the well-used interior with its creaking old floorboards. To them the wheel on the landing, which in the past had been used to set and release the brake, was a steering wheel, that they would do their best to turn. They enjoyed pretending to drive the old Blue Imp Fire Truck, that had been placed on the playground; each taking her turn as the driver. Pa was always relegated to ride in the back seat where he would be chauffeured to imaginary fires.

But the highlight of every trip to the park, the main reason for the outing and the first thing on our agenda, was to feed the birds. During the summer months there was always an assortment of tame ducks and geese, and occasionally we even saw wild mallards, on the pond. The excitement meter rose to extreme whenever the girls were able to feed the ducks and geese.

The first stop on our adventure was always at the IGA in Stony Plain, where we would pick up a loaf of the freshest day-old bread. We knew from past experience that the Stony Plain ducks and geese just loved the freshest day-old IGA bread.

The excitement started to build as we entered the store. Megan and Amy charged through the door and raced ahead to the counter where the day-old bread was displayed. When I arrived at the counter, I was greeted by two of the longest, saddest faces I had ever seen. They both turned and looked at me, and I could see the disappointment in their eyes.

"Look, Pa!" Amy said, as she pointed to the counter.

"Pa, there's no bread," Megan said.

It was a sad scene, to say the least, as they both stood there looking at the empty counter. The unasked question was written all over their little faces: What would we feed the geese?

"That old counter looks pretty bare, doesn't it?" I said.

"What are we going to do, Pa?" Amy asked.

"I don't know, what do you girls think we should do?"

"We have to find some day-old bread," Amy said, and her voice was very serious. "The gooses are hungry, aren't they, Pa?"

"Well, it has been a while since we were at the pond the last time," I said, "so I suspect that those geese will be getting hungry all right."

"We could feed them something else, couldn't we, Pa?" Megan asked.

"That's a good idea, Megan," I said. "Why don't you girls look around the store and pick out what you think you'd like to eat if you were a hungry goose."

"Really?" Amy replied, as if she couldn't believe what she had just heard.

"Okay," Megan said, as she immediately seized the opportunity. "Amy, what would you like to eat if you were a goose?"

Oh, there was a considerable amount of very serious thought and deliberation that went into the decision as we strolled through the aisles and searched the shelves for just the right goose food. The chocolate-bar section drew some very serious consideration. But we moved on. Finally it was agreed that if the girls were geese, they would both like to have a hot-dog bun. And so it was that on this day, the lucky geese at the Dog Rump Creek Park in Stony Plain were going to have a real treat—fresh hot-dog buns.

The excitement meter continued to rise as we drove into the park. The geese must have sensed the arrival of fresh hot-dog buns, for they reacted immediately when we drove into the parking area. They had been lazing on the water but quickly moved towards shore. Their wings were flapping like crazy, and they were paddling their feet rapidly as they hefted their huge bodies out of the water. Then dirt and grass flew as they clawed their way up the bank and, honking expectantly, they hurriedly waddled across the mowed grass towards the car. It was as if they sensed there was a good surprise in store for them. Each one was obviously looking for the first share of the fresh hot-dog buns.

One big old gander led the welcoming committee. Waddling as fast as he could, that old gander waddled ahead and arrived at the car about a dozen waddles ahead of his flock. He was there to greet us before we had a chance to step out of the car. That big old gander seemed to know that the early bird gets the worm — or, in this case, the fresh hot-dog bun.

Now, in all honesty it must be said that Nanna, too, loved to feed the birds at the pond. And it just may have been a toss-up as to who enjoyed the experience more, Nanna or the girls. However, on this day it was Nanna who was carrying the feed bag when we got out of the car. To our surprise, Nanna rewarded that old gander for his efforts.

"Here, girl," Nanna said, incorrectly identifying the sex of the old boy, and then, much to the girls' horror, she ripped a piece off a fresh hot-dog bun and flipped it to that lead goose. Although feeding the geese at the car was one of the no-no's, it wasn't entirely unexpected, for we all knew that Nanna could not stand to see the first goose that arrived on the scene go without one little crumb of whatever we had to feed them. I stood back and smiled, for I knew full well the reaction that was to follow.

"Nanna, you're not supposed to do that," Amy said, scolding Nanna as only Amy can do.

"Why? What's wrong with giving that poor old goose one little crumb?" Nanna replied. "Look at her, that poor goose is hungry."

"Because Pa said you're not supposed to feed the geese until Amy and I are up on the top of one of the picnic tables, Nanna!" Megan said, reminding Nanna of the rule.

"Remember, Nanna?" Amy said, and she was dead serious as she reminded Nanna of the one rule we had when feeding the geese. "Pa said you're not supposed to give the gooses anything to eat until Megan and I are on top of the table. Or else they might bite us with their beaks."

"I know. I know," Nanna replied, acknowledging her indiscretion as the rest of the flock were arriving on the scene. "I just gave her one little crumb. Look how hungry she is, she gobbled it down like a pig. One little crumb can't hurt."

"Pa said the gooses might fly at us and bite us," Amy said as the arriving flock made a beeline for Nanna and the fresh hot-dog buns.

"What can it hurt if I give them only one crumb?" Nanna said, pooh-poohing the idea and the rule.

The geese were ignoring everyone but Nanna. She suddenly found herself to be a very popular person as hungry geese surrounded her. They were crowding around Nanna, all hoping to get their share of the hot-dog buns.

Megan tried to reason with Nanna. "Pa says that he's seen geese attack little kids—and sometimes even grown-ups—who have food or even bags in their hands. Pa says that geese can be mean. Pa says that geese have learned that if they run at people flapping their wings and honking like crazy, then people have to run for their lives until they drop whatever they have in their hands. Pa says that if the people don't drop the food they're carrying, then the geese will peck them. Pa says that geese have strong beaks and they're really sharp. They can really hurt you, especially if you're just a little kid."

The geese were showing signs of losing their patience. They were now beginning to crowd Nanna, forcing her to hold the bag of fresh hot-dogs buns at eye level to avoid the snapping beaks. Nanna was not about to be one of the people who dropped her bag of food and ran for her life.

"Yeah, and me and Megan, we don't want to get attacked by a mean geese," Amy continued the scolding as the geese swarmed Nanna, sandwiching her between feathered, insistent bodies that were now pushing up against her legs. "Pa says, them gooses aren't dumb, you know, Nanna."

My goodness, I thought, and smiled to myself, that was almost word for word. I couldn't have said that better myself. I now had it first-hand that at least someone was listening to what I had to say.

"I'm sorry! I'm sorry," Nanna quickly responded. "Meia culpa. Meia culpa. I won't do it again. But you know, girls, Pa doesn't know everything!" she said and then added under her breath, "He just thinks he does."

At this point, Nanna was holding the bread as high above her head as she could, trying to avoid the aggressive birds.

"Okay, girls," I said, "let's head for our picnic table."

The girls needed no further encouragement; they both turned and raced ahead. Nanna and her entourage, the flock of geese, were in hot pursuit as they hustled

those birds in the eye, as long as they're standing firmly on the ground. As we have already established, the geese knew where the fresh hot-dog buns were and who was carrying them. And when it came to fresh hot-dog buns, those geese were not patient waiters. When Nanna quickened her step, those poor old geese were not able to keep up, even though they too had shifted their slow waddling gear into their fastest waddling gait. Nanna started to pull away, but not for long. The geese needed help, and as if on cue, they all honked at once, then spread their wings, flapping wildly to make up the lost ground. I had seen Nanna and flying birds on many occasions, and I could see the panic that gripped her face when she glanced over at the first goose that flapped up alongside of her. A frightened Nanna shifted into high gear and took off like a scared rabbit. However, Nanna still had a problem for the faster Nanna ran the harder the geese flapped their wings, in an effort to keep up with her. And the harder the geese flapped their wings, the faster an absolutely terrified Nanna ran, in her effort to escape from them. Once more she shifted gears, and this time she shifted into overdrive. Now Nanna was really motoring.

The girls, safe on the top of the picnic table, watched in awe, speechless. In my customary place, bringing up the rear, I had the best seat in the house, so to speak—and if I may say so, it was an entertaining performance that streaked across the park ahead of me.

Nanna was near out-of-control panic by the time she and the flapping, honking flock arrived at the picnic table. She hesitated for a second, and I was sure that she was going to vault onto that picnic table, but she didn't. Apparently she thought better of that idea, as her best vaulting days were definitely behind her. Instead, she plunked the plastic bag with the fresh hot-dog buns onto the top of the table, where Megan and Amy stood in stunned silence, and without slowing down, she darted right on past the table, even though she was now empty-handed.

When the bag disappeared from her hand, the geese slammed on the brakes. Immediately the flapping stopped, as the geese milled around and honked noisily as they searched for the bag of fresh hot-dog buns. The danger at last seemed to be over, and a breathless Nanna stopped and uttered a sigh of relief.

"Holy!" declared a gasping Nanna as she struggled to catch her breath. "I don't know what's got into those crazy geese."

Meanwhile some of the geese were trying to see up onto the top of the table. Some were searching under the table and under the bench seats. But the old gander, not convinced that Nanna was no longer the source of that delicious bun, waddled over to her and was carefully checking her out.

Megan and Amy quickly forgot about the chase. They each scooped a bun out of the bag and busied themselves tearing off little chunks of hot-dog bun that they flipped to the hungry, exhausted birds. Sometimes the girls flipped pieces to the geese that crowded around the table; sometimes they tossed pieces to the ducks that had stayed swimming around the edge of the pond during Nanna's mad dash across the grass.

With the fear of flapping geese gone, Nanna ignored the old gander; she stepped up to the table and picked up a hot-dog bun. Having resisted the earlier urge to vault onto the table, Nanna now planted her feet firmly on the ground. She was smiling happily as she began tearing off little pieces of bun and was hand-feeding the honking birds that were once more closing in around her.

The excitement of the race was over, and I stood to one side where I could watch Megan and Amy.

Suddenly, from behind me, there was a blood-curdling screech. Instinctively I flinched and ducked as I spun around to face the danger. I was just in time to see another sight unfold.

The old gander, the one who had received the first treat back at the car, must have found what he had been searching for. He had his head and beak up under the back side of Nanna's shorts. And obviously he had a beakful, for he was twisting and turning his beak viciously from side to side, trying his best to tear off his share. At the same time Nanna, in a futile attempt to shake him loose, executed several fancy, never-before-seen dance steps — or they could have been some new fangled aerobic moves. I wasn't sure. Then, with all the agility of an expert in the martial arts, Nanna spun around and gave that old gander a vicious karate chop to the side of his beak, all the while holding onto her chunk of hot-dog bun. Instantly the ganders eyelids snapped shut and I thought she had killed the old boy. Unfortunately for Nanna, the old gander had only blinked and, before she could react, his eyelids popped

130

open, and with renewed vigor he again tried to tear away a hunk of rump. For his efforts, he received another solid karate chop to the head that forced him to let go.

"Ouch!" Nanna screamed again. "Bad goose! That hurts, you know!" A pained expression creased her face as she scolded the old gander.

It appeared to me that the old gander had gone sort of cross-eyed after that last blow; however, he recovered quickly and he ignored both the karate chop and the tongue-lashing. The gander's one good eye was focused on that hand which was at the end of her outstretched arm, high above her head. Nanna rubbed her butt vigorously with her free hand while maintaining a firm grip on the remnants of the fresh hot-dog bun. Nanna's eyes were blinking rapidly as the ravenous goose flapped his wings like crazy and craned his neck in a desperate attempt to get at the bun. But Nanna was a trooper; she kept the bun out of reach.

"Are you having a little goose trouble, Nanna?" I asked.

"That — that big goose, it — it just bit Nanna on the bum," Amy said, and her eyes were as big as saucers.

"Pa, that big goose stuck his beak right up under Nanna's shorts and bit her on the bum," Megan said and nodded her head, agreeing with Amy.

"No! Did it really?" I said, trying to appear to be shocked, while at the same time stifling a chuckle.

"Yes, it did, Pa. It bit Nanna right on the bum," Amy said, confirming Megan's diagnosis.

At that point Nanna had had enough of hand-feeding the geese, especially the one that was now giving her a cross-eyed look and flapping his wings in her face. Still rubbing her butt, she unceremoniously hauled herself up onto the top of the table to get out of reach of the lecherous beak.

"Are you all right Nanna? Or would you like me to examine the injured part?" I asked.

"No, I wouldn't," she snorted.

"Nanna, you should listen to Pa," Megan quickly chimed in. "Pa said you shouldn't feed the geese until you are standing on the table."

"See Nanna?" Amy said to her in all innocence. "Pa is smart, and he does know everything."

I tried, but I could no longer stifle the chuckle as I watched Nanna rub her sore butt.

Aren't grandkids the greatest!

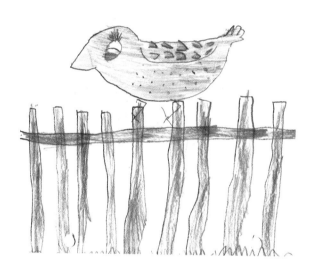

"LOOK AT ME, PA!"

The swimming pool at the Jasper Inn has become a real favourite for Megan and Amy. For the past five years Nanna and I have taken the girls to Jasper for a few days in July or August. What started out to be a one-time experience on the train has become an annual event at the Jasper Inn—in particular the pool—a summer holiday unto itself. Kelly tells me that when she is planning anything at all for the summer holidays, both Megan and Amy ask right away: "Is it the same time as our trip to Jasper?" Nothing is more important than, or interferes with, our annual trek west on the train to the magnificent Canadian Rockies.

*   *   *   *   *

Taking our granddaughters on a train ride to Jasper was the result of reliving some of my childhood experiences. The train journey was something that I had

134

planned to do; I just hadn't as yet set the date. Then I came across a newspaper article that really got the ball rolling. The article was about a cross-country Canadian adventure that someone had recently taken on Canada's only surviving passenger train, Via Rail, and it got me to thinking.

The first thing that came to mind was a rumour making the rounds that VIA Rail Canada might be shutting down, discontinuing the only passenger-train service in Canada. Immediately I had a sentimental moment as I thought of what that meant to me.

Gone would be the mode of travel that, when I was a little boy, linked the Atlantic coast to the Pacific coast of Canada and all points in between. Gone would be the mighty iron beasts that I used to stand in awe of as they chugged and puffed into the CNR station in Edson, or that I heard as they screamed and rattled through the woodlands. Gone would be the main link in the chain that united our nation from sea to sea and played such an important role in the development of our great country.

"You know, Nanna," I said as I put the article aside, "some of my best memories are from those early days and the trips that I took on the passenger train when I was a little boy. And now it sounds like the passenger train may soon disappear from the prairies as did the passenger pigeon. Like so many other things, the passenger train in Canada could be just another part of history that my grandchildren can only read about, or see in a museum."

For a moment my mind drifted back — back to the

1940s. It was a time when the train was an important, if not the most important, mode of transportation in Canada. To a country boy, it seemed as if everybody rode the train. Unless a person walked, the train was the only sure way of getting from one place to another at all times of the year. The train was always there and it was always on time. I could never remember it being late.

In fact, for many people, the train was their clock, so regular was the train schedule, and if you happened to be one of the fortunate few who did have a watch back then, you could have set it by the trains arrival in your town.

Even now, I can see myself as a little boy on a passenger train that is racing through the foothills of Alberta. The picture is so clear: I'm standing beside the side door, and the window is open. I can feel the cool breeze as it whistles around me, knotting and tangling my hair, driving black coal cinders right down to my scalp. Mom would be furious when I got home — she was never happy with me coming home with my hair full of coal fines. I loved the clickety-clack of the iron wheels on the rails, the chugging of the steam engine, and the scream of the steam whistle as the train roared across the countryside.

From the Stump Farm I couldn't see the train, but I could always hear it: the scream of the steam whistle announcing the arrival of every train, and the chug-chug-chug as the engine laboured to pull away from the station. It would be a sad day if the trains were gone tomorrow and my granddaughters had never experienced the thrill of a train ride.

"Isn't that too bad," Nanna said. Her reply broke the spell and brought me back to the article.

"No, it's sad. A real shame. You know, Nanna, every Canadian should really experience a train ride, at least once in their life, even if it is for only one day. And I think that I would like to take Megan and Amy on that train ride," I said. "I would like for them to experience the type of thrills that I had when I was a boy, riding on the train."

"That would be nice. Where do you want to take them?" she asked.

"I don't know," I replied. And suddenly I felt a twinge of sadness and a lump in my throat as I continued. "It's been a long time since I rode on a train. Too long. There have been so many changes—drastic cuts to the passenger services. I don't even know where the passenger train runs anymore."

Then, as I have been known to do, I forgot about the train; as my life, the life of a happily retired man, returned to other things. But Nanna, bless her soul, had not forgotten about the train. If there was a chance to do something, anything, with the girls I could count on her to lead the charge. The next night, at supper, she surprised me.

"I can get us tickets on VIA to go to Jasper for three days in July," Nanna said. "I put a hold on them until tomorrow night."

"That's high season in Jasper," I said. "Where would we stay? I doubt that we'll find a place this late in the year."

"I can get us a suite with one bedroom and a three bed loft at the Jasper Inn for those days," Nanna said.

"You can, at this time of the year?" I asked.

"Yes, I can," Nanna replied. "I spoke to the General Manager, Shawnee, this morning, and she's put a room on hold for me. She said they're really busy, so I have to let them know by tomorrow if we're coming."

"That's great! Good job, Nanna," I said. "But you'll have to call Kelly and make sure it's all right with her."

"Kelly said those dates are good. She thinks the girls might enjoy the train ride."

"We'll need a car as well, so that we can go and see some of the sights and the animals," I said.

"I've tentatively booked a car for the whole time we're there. We just have to phone them when we get into the station in Jasper, and they'll deliver it," Nanna said.

"Fantastic! You've thought of everything," I said.

"I just need to know if that's what you want to do."

"Book it, Nanna," I replied happily. "Book it. We're going to have a ball."

Everything went as planned. We met Kelly and Bill and our granddaughters at the train station in Edmonton. Megan and Amy were just as excited as I had hoped they would be. They pulled their little suitcases behind them wherever they ran—and they ran all over the station, checking out every corner.

Time seemed to fly, and before we knew it, we had boarded the train. As we walked forward towards our coach, I could see Kelly and Bill following along, monitoring our progress. Outside on the platform they matched us stride for stride. Being the first in line did have its benefits, and we were able to select our seats and get a table.

"Look, girls," I said. "Who's that standing outside the train beside our window?"

"It's Mommy and Daddy," they both seemed to call out at the same time, and they each rushed to the window and pressed their noses against the glass.

It was at that point that the tears came. Great big tears welled up in the eyes before streaming down the cheeks, as the realization of what was happening hit home. Megan and Amy were going on a trip without Mommy and Daddy. It was the first time the girls were having a holiday and Mommy and Daddy were staying at home. It was a new and traumatic experience for everyone.

"How come Mommy's crying?" Megan asked.

"Oh, I think she's just happy that you girls are going on your first train ride," I replied.

"Do big people always cry when they're happy?" she asked.

"Sometimes they do," I said.

"Mommy must be really happy," Amy said, "'cause she's really crying."

As the train slowly pulled out of the station, Kelly and Bill began to move. They walked along on the platform, staying right beside our window, keeping up with our coach. At first they walked slowly, but they picked up the pace as the train gathered speed, and finally they were racing along at a good clip when they ran out of platform. They stopped, and the train roared away toward the Rocky Mountains, Jasper, and a whole new experience.

"Mommy's still crying," Amy said as Kelly and Bill disappeared.

"Yes, she is, Buddy," I replied. "I guess she must really be happy that you're going on the train."

Actually, I was surprised that Kelly was able to see the platform through all the water she was shedding.

"The train will be going through Spruce Grove in a couple of minutes," I said when we crossed the trestle east of town.

"Do you think we can see our house from the train when we go through Spruce Grove?" Megan asked.

"I don't know," I replied. "I guess we'll have to look carefully and see."

The train never even slowed down as we rolled into town.

"There's our car!" Amy yelled. "I see Mommy and Daddy!"

"Oh, I don't think so, Amy. They're probably still in Edmonton," I said as I looked ahead.

But Amy was right—there they were, standing beside their car at the first crossing in Spruce Grove. Kelly was waving frantically, and the tears were still flowing freely as the train roared past.

"Don't tell me we're going to see them at every railway crossing between here and Jasper," I said to Mar.

We checked out the next two crossings, but they were both empty. There were no cars parked next to the tracks. There were no more tears, and we were able to get on with our holiday.

The girls were thrilled with the train ride. Their favorite place on the train was the dining car—it was also my favorite when I was a child—and they loved the dome car. Sadly, passenger trains didn't have dome cars in my day.

From the dome car the girls could see the whole countryside, on both sides of the train. The train snaked through the foothills, where the skies became overcast, and thick, heavy, dark clouds spat the occasional rain shower. In the Obed Hills the girls saw a large black bear at the edge of the forest. The train rolled through Hinton and into the Rocky Mountains, and the girls became very silent. They sat in awe, staring out and up through the rain-splattered windows of the dome car at the majestic Rockies towering above them.

It was not a nice day in Jasper; a cold wind and rain greeted us as we stepped down from the train. Megan and Amy were not impressed with the weather. However, the weather was all but forgotten when we arrived at the Jasper Inn and they discovered the swimming pools. The pools were indoors, away from the clouds, the wind, and the rain. There was a large pool, with warm water. There was a kids' paddling pool, with slightly warmer water. There was a hot tub, with even warmer water. And there was a sauna and a steam room.

It was paradise on a cold, windy, rainy day. The outside world melted away as the girls waded into the pool for the first time. Neither of them could swim when we arrived at the hotel that year. They were confined to the kids' pool. As the years went by, however, Megan gained confidence and became an excellent swimmer, abandoning Nanna and Amy in the kids' pool and joining me in the big pool.

*   *   *   *   *

On our latest trip to Jasper, Megan was swimming like a fish. Amy, a free spirit, was still content to be running between the kids' pool and the hot tub with Nanna, the other non-swimmer. But there were changes in the air. Amy was on the cusp of leaving Nanna behind to soak in the shallow waters of the kids' pool, alone.

"Look at me, Pa!" Amy cried. She was in the kids' pool, and only her little head was above the water. "Look at me, Pa, I'm swimming!"

I looked down at the happy little face in the kids' pool. Yes, her head was above the water and the rest of her below. Her eyes were wide open with excitement, and in the deep blue water her blond hair looked almost white. She was kicking, and her arms were flailing wildly as she thrashed about, trying to stay afloat. She was struggling to keep her head bobbing above the surface of the water in the kids' pool. Her little legs, with her knees bent like pretzels, were pumping and kicking frantically in the water below her body. Her little arms were stretched out as far as they could go as she paddled. Her delicate fingers were spread out, and it appeared that she was reaching for the bottom of the pool, which was just beyond her grasp. My Lord, I thought as I watched her dog-paddle, it must be an inherent trait, for I myself am a dog-paddler from way back, as was my father before me.

"Wow, just look at you go," I said, and I smiled as only a proud grandfather can smile when a milestone has been reached.

She soaked up my encouragement, beaming with pride and grinning from ear to ear, forgetting to keep her mouth closed and swallowing more than her share of the water in the kids' pool. I was happy to have a part in Amy learning to swim.

After watching Amy dog-paddle for a bit, I turned back to the big pool to see how Megan was doing. It was right here at the Jasper Inn only a few summers ago, that Megan had actually began to swim, and now, she was swimming like an otter. I was bursting with pride at her accomplishments, having been a huge part of the learning process.

Yes, there she was, at the bottom of the pool in five feet of water. Since Megan had learned to swim, she spent more of her swimming time at the bottom of the pool than at the top. As I looked down at her, she kicked off and shot to the top. Her head broke the surface near where I stood.

"Hi, Pa," Megan said and smiled.

Then she took a big gulp of air and, as cool as a cucumber and without a worry in the world, she flipped over and once more headed back down. I dove under the water to watch as she descended, and when she sat down on the bottom of the pool, I came for air.

"Look at me, Pa!" I heard Amy call as my head burst

through the surface of the pool. "Look at me! I can swim."

I forgot about Megan, wiped the water from my face, and took a casual glance over at the kids' paddling pool. My heart skipped a beat and I just about died right there—the kids' paddling pool was empty. I frantically looked around to see where the voice had come from, and to my horror, found the source in the big pool. There, at the deep end of the pool in five feet of water, was Amy's little head. It was bobbing around on the top of the water while the rest of the body was thrashing frantically to keep it there. Her eyes were full of pride and excitement. They were glistening like a couple of crystal balls, and her face held a grin that was full of determination. Although there was a tremendous amount of energy being spent, she was making very little headway swimming. Her mouth was open and she was once more swallowing more than her share of water. She was trying desperately to paddle her way across the big pool to where I was, or drink the pool dry—which ever came first.

"Go back, Amy!" I yelled. "Go back! You can't swim!"

"Yes I can! Look at me, Pa! Look at me! I'm swimming!"

Sometimes I think that without my love for the passenger train, my granddaughters would never have learned to swim.

144

IT'S YOUR CHOICE

When Megan successfully completed Grade One, Nanna invited her to a sleepover celebration. With Amy, of course. The girls come as a package, never one without the other. Not wanting to be outdone, I offered to take them all out for supper.

The girls arrived, each with her own little suitcase—one green and yellow, the other one red and yellow. In a flash of colour they raced up the driveway as fast as their little legs would carry them, pulling their suitcases behind them.

"Where would you like to go for your special supper?" I asked Megan as soon as the girls had deposited their suitcases in the bedroom.

Imagine my surprise when she chose one of Nanna's and my favorite Chinese restaurants. Mind you, it is also a favourite of both girls. They look forward to seeing Mr. Woo, the manager, who always makes a big fuss over them; he even remembers their names, as well as their favourite Chinese dishes. As he always does, Mr. Woo met us at the door.

"Hello, Megan," he said, greeting her.

"Hello," Megan replied shyly.

Then he turned to Amy and he paused deliberately. There was just a trace of a little wrinkle that creased his brow, and we could all tell that he was thinking very hard. A little worry frown developed on Amy's forehead as she waited expectantly. Suddenly a big smile lit up Mr. Woos face.

"Hello, Amy," he said, almost warbling the words.

"Hi," Amy replied, and just as quickly the worry frown was gone. Thank goodness Mr. Woo hadn't forgotten her name.

"What can I have, Pa?" Megan asked before Mr. Woo had even counted out four menus.

I was sort of taken by surprise, for it was not like Megan to ask for anything outright. She was always so reserved and polite. Normally I would have to ask her what she wanted, and then wait for a reply as she contemplated her options. But not on that day. She took the lead and asked her question before we had been shown to our table. In fact, it seemed as if we had barely walked through the door.

"Well," I began, and I hesitated. "Let me think, now. You just passed from Grade One to Grade Two, didn't you?"

"Uh-huh," Megan said and nodded her head up and

147

down. I could see by the look in her eyes that she was waiting with great anticipation for my answer.

"Well, then, in that case, Megan, you can have whatever you want," I said, with all the confidence in the world that she would choose one of her favourites—the Vietnamese spring rolls, or the deep-fried crispy won tons—and if not one of these favourites, she would surely opt for the deep-fried pork chops with salt and pepper. "It's your choice."

Megan's eyes said it all. They were alive, sparkling like crystals in a cool, clear mountain stream. She gave me a smile that lit up the room and warmed my heart. It was the answer she had hoped for, and I hadn't disappointed her. I just about popped the buttons off my shirt, I felt so proud.

Mr. Woo suddenly seemed to get into the mood too; he stood there and nodded approvingly at my offer. An expectant smile lit up his face.

"Really, Pa? Whatever I'd like?" she asked.

"Really, buddy. It's your choice."

"I'll have a lobster, Pa," she said as nonchalantly as if having lobster were just another ordinary, every day occurrence.

I stopped short. I hadn't thought of lobster as even being on the menu. We had certainly never ordered lobster.

Then I looked at Mr. Woo. I don't think he had thought of lobster either, but he was certainly thinking of it now as he looked at the four of us standing in the entrance. Suddenly the smile that he had been sporting faded and was replaced with a look of concern. His eyes darted past us to the lobster tank. I watched his head bob slightly as he counted the lobsters in the tank. I quickly turned and counted them too. There were five. He breathed a sigh of relief, and I swallowed hard. When he turned back to me, I could have sworn I saw little dollar signs in his eyes, and now his face was bursting with a smile that was even bigger than Megan's.

"Oh, well . . . uh, have you ever eaten lobster, buddy?" I asked, trying to find the right words. I was wondering where in the world Megan had come up with the idea to have lobster, and how the word had even made its way into her vocabulary.

"No," she replied innocently, and continued to smile at me confidently. She knew that I wouldn't disappoint her.

"Maybe we should look at the menu and then decide," I said.

"The lobster is a very good choice," Mr. Woo said, and his voice had a little triumphant ring to it. "And we do have lots of lobster."

"If I get you a lobster, are you going to eat it all?" I asked Megan.

"Uh-huh," she replied, and once more she nodded her head. Mr. Woo was also nodding his head approvingly.

"Okay, that's settled, then," I said. "It sounds like Megan is going to have lobster tonight."

"Is everybody going to have lobster?" asked Mr. Woo, who was having a hard time believing his good luck, and now he was rubbing his hands together, like a person who had just won the lottery.

"I don't know," I said. "Nanna, do you want a lobster?"

Mr. Woo was rapidly nodding his head, signalling that he was voting yes.

"I'm just going to have an egg roll and some beef and broccoli," Nanna replied.

"What about you," I asked Amy, "would you like to have lobster too?"

Again Mr. Woo had an expectant look on his face. I was sure that he, like me, fully expected Amy to follow in the footsteps of her big sister.

"I want a hot dog," Amy replied. Once more the smile was fading from Mr. Woo's face.

Hotdog, I thought, why in the world would she ask for a hot dog in a Chinese restaurant? Amy had always ordered the deep-fried wontons.

"We don't have hot dogs," Mr. Woo quickly chimed in, as he shook his head vigorously to emphasize the point. "We have lobster! Why don't you all come over to the lobster tank and check out the lobster?" The smile returned to his face as he pointed toward the lobster tank.

"I don't like lobster," Amy said, almost destroying the poor man.

"Have you ever had lobster?" I asked Amy.

"No," she said. "I want a hot dog."

Unlike Megan, who hadn't yet tried lobster either, Amy obviously wasn't ready to acquire a taste for the finer things in life.

"Amy wants a hot dog," I said to Mr. Woo.

"We don't have hot dog," Mr. Woo repeated.

"I wonder where we can get a lobster and a hot dog," I mused for Mr. Woo's benefit, and to reassure Amy that she, too, was special.

"I get you a hot dog," Mr. Woo quickly chimed in. "Hot dog no problem."

"I didn't think so," I said. "Then, Mr. Woo, it looks like we'll have one lobster and one hot dog, and Nanna and I will order off the menu. Megan, why don't you go with Mr. Woo and pick out your lobster."

Mr. Woo showed Nanna and myself to our booth, then led Megan over to the lobster tank. But Amy wasn't going to be left out. She may not have wanted to eat lobster, but she wasn't about to pass up the opportunity to get a close-up look at those lobsters.

"What are we going to do if she doesn't eat it?" Nanna asked me.

I just smiled, for I had a real good idea what we were going to do if Megan didn't eat her lobster.

While Nanna and I talked, I saw Megan pointing at her supper in the lobster tank. Then the girls stood back and watched as Mr. Woo and a waiter snagged the lobster that Megan had pointed to.

It wasn't long before the trio came racing back to our table. Mr. Woo, carrying the granddaddy of all live lobsters, was ecstatic. He looked as if he still couldn't believe this was happening when he showed me the lobster that Megan had selected. After all, who in their right mind orders a six-year-old child a lobster? Megan's eyes were still open wide, and the grin had not left her little face. There was no doubt in my mind that she knew which string to pull; she had my number and she was about to get her first lobster.

Amy was staring in disbelief at Megan's lobster. She leaned in for a closer look. There was something about the scratching sounds that the lobster's claws made on the plate in its futile struggle to get away that fascinated her. She couldn't seem to take her eyes off those claws.

"Is this lobster okay?" asked Mr. Woo as he presented the huge live lobster to me.

"Well, now, I'm not sure. That's a pretty big lobster for a little girl," I said, and the poor man's face sagged. "Is this the lobster you picked out?" I asked Megan.

"Uh-huh," she replied.

"Are you sure you can eat it all?" I asked again, just to make sure.

"Uh-huh," she said.

"And was this the smallest lobster in the tank?" I asked.

"No, it wasn't!" Amy suddenly blurted out. "It was the biggest one, Pa. Megan picked the biggest lobster in the tank!"

"Did you, buddy?" I asked.

"Uh-huh," she said. I didn't think her smile could get any bigger, but it did.

"Then, I guess that lobster is okay," I said. With that, Mr. Woo spun around like a top and hustled out to the kitchen.

"I don't think he sells many lobsters," Nanna said. "He didn't even stop to take our orders."

"He probably wants to get it into the boiling water before I change my mind," I said and chuckled.

But to our surprise, Mr. Woo came hustling back across the restaurant, still carrying the live lobster on the plate. For some reason, the lobster was more active, and it was making a lot of scratching noise on the plate. Amy was still fascinated and stood up to get a better look.

"This lobster will cost you forty-two dollars and seventy-nine cents," Mr. Woo said. He almost looked sad as he gave me the news. I'm sure he thought the deal was off.

"Really! You wouldn't want to throw in the seventy-nine cents, would you?" I said jokingly, then I winked at him.

"No! No!" he quickly replied in a very serious tone.

"I was only kidding, Mr. Woo," I said. My obvious attempt at humour was completely lost on Mr. Woo.

"This lobster is going to cost you forty-two dollars and seventy-nine cents," he said, putting the emphasis on the seventy-nine cents. Poor Mr. Woo wore a sickly smile, and I'm sure he was hoping that the deal was still on.

I recognized immediately that with a forty-two-dollar-and-seventy-nine-cent lobster at stake, he had suddenly lost his sense of humour.

"You still want the lobster?" he asked.

"We sure do, don't we, buddy?" I said to Megan. She smiled and nodded her head. "Throw it in the pot and boil it up, Mr. Woo."

A relieved Mr. Woo raced the lobster away to the

kitchen, just in case I decided to change my mind.

Mr. Woo hovered over the table during our meal. He snapped the tail off the lobster, ignoring the steam that had to be burning his hands, and removed the meat. He helped Megan crack the claws and legs. Mr. Woo was an expert at salvaging the edible portions of lobster meat that lay hidden within the shell. When he was finished, Mr. Woo had extracted every morsel of that lobster, even the very hard-to-get meat in the tiny legs.

When the meal was over, I looked at my bill. The lobster was forty-two dollars and seventy-nine cents; the total bill was sixty-three dollars and eleven cents. And Megan had eaten every single bite of her first lobster.

Now, three years later, we are about to celebrate Amy's accomplishment. She has just finished her first year in school; she, too, has passed from Grade One into Grade Two. As tradition dictated, the girls were having a sleepover at Nanna and Pa's house, and I had made the same offer to Amy. As soon as their little suitcases were stashed safely in the bedroom, we met downstairs.

"Well, buddy, it's your choice. We'll go wherever you want for supper, and you can have whatever you want," I said and awaited her decision, wondering what exotic choices she would make.

Amy looked at me for the longest time. I could almost hear the gears in her little head as she sorted through all the options. In the past three years we had taken the girls to many restaurants, so Amy's options were not as limited as Megan's had been. Amy was taking her time as she made her choice. She knew that she could go wherever and she could have whatever she wanted. There was no doubt that she was giving the whole process some deep thought and very serious consideration before she spoke.

"I want to stay here, at your house, Pa," she said confidently. "And I want a hotdog!"

Some things never change.

THE BRIGHT GREEN HARP

"Hi, Dad." It was my daughter Kelly on the phone. "Megan wants to ask you a question," she said, and I could feel the excitement in her voice.

I loved it when I heard that tone, for it meant that I was going to be asked to do something important, something special, with one or both of my granddaughters. In my mind I was rapidly thinking of where I could take them for lunch the next day, since many of the requests were of that nature. But regardless of what the request might be, it meant that I would be spending some quality time with them, without the interference of insensitive parents.

"Okay," I replied and eagerly waited while the phone changed hands.

"Pa." It was Megan's voice. She sounded so meek and tentative.

"Yes, buddy, it's me," I replied. I hoped that I had the right tone in my voice to give her confidence to ask me anything.

"Pa, can you help me build an instrument?" she asked.

"An instrument?" I said. I was rather taken aback, for making an instrument wasn't at all what I had expected. "What do you need an instrument for?"

"It's a school project, Pa," she said, "and all the grade threes have to make a musical instrument for school."

"Oh. Well, sure, buddy," I said. I knew that Megan and I could whip up an instrument for her Grade three class. For sure something like a Kleenex-box guitar or a willow flute could be made in no time flat. "We can build a nice little guitar. Hmm, let me see, now. I think we can use a Kleenex box, a cardboard tube—you know, like the ones that gift wrap or paper towels come on—and some string. That shouldn't be too hard."

There was dead silence on the other end of the line. I waited for an answer that never came, and I began to think that maybe my guitar idea was not that good.

"Would a guitar like that be okay?" I finally asked, hoping for an enthusiastic *yes*.

"Well, I—I guess so," came her hesitant, reluctant response.

I knew from the way her answer came back that I was already on my way to blowing the class project. The Kleenex-box guitar was not what she had in mind.

I could feel the disappointment in her voice; it hung heavy on the phone. But Megan was just too nice, too polite a little girl. No matter how badly she might have wanted something different, if a Kleenex-box guitar was what Pa wanted to help her build, she would agree to it rather than hurt my feelings.

"Did you want Pa to help you build a fancy guitar, instead of one out of a Kleenex box?" I asked.

"No . . . no . . ., that's okay," she said. "The Kleenex-box guitar would be fine, I guess." The hesitation in her voice told me I was out in left field with my suggestions.

"Well then, I'll bet that you don't want to make a guitar at all. Do you, buddy?" I asked.

"No," she said rather meekly, "but that's okay, we can build a Kleenex-box guitar."

"Did you want Pa to help you build a flute, like the whistles I make out of a willow stick?" I asked. "You know, I'm a pretty good whistle-whittler."

There was a long pause while she considered the willow whistle.

"No," she finally said in a very weak voice.

"What did you have in mind, buddy?" I asked, because at this point I had used up all of my worldly music-making-instrument talents.

"I was wondering if you could help me make a harp," she said.

"A harp?" I blurted out.

"Uh-huh."

Where had a harp come from, I thought. Why, I had never heard anyone in our family even talk about a

159

harp, let alone want to make one. How in the world did one go about making a harp? I needed help on this one.

"Could I speak to your Mommy?" I asked.

"Mom, Pa wants to speak to you," I heard Megan call to Kelly.

"Is Pa going to help you make a harp?" I heard Kelly ask Megan in the background.

"I don't know," Megan replied.

"Well, didn't you ask him?"

"Uh-huh."

"What did he say?"

"Nothing. He said he wants to speak to you."

"Nothing! He said nothing!" Kelly exclaimed, as if she couldn't believe what she was hearing.

"Speak to me, Kelly," I mumbled into the receiver. "I need some help here."

"Hey, old guy, what's the problem? Don't you want to help your granddaughter build a harp?" I could feel the cutting edge in that comment.

"A harp," I said. "She wants me to help her build a harp!"

"I know," Kelly replied. "It was her idea. That's what she wants to build. Don't you want to help her?"

Now I felt like I was getting the old guilt trip.

"I would love to help her," I replied quickly, "but I need some help. I have absolutely no idea how to go about building a harp. In fact, I don't even really know what a harp looks like, other than it's very large."

"Don't worry, Megan knows how to build a harp. She knows exactly what she wants. She has already drawn it out on a piece of paper. She'll do most of the work. She just needs you to help her cut the wood out and glue the pieces together."

"Oh well, in that case, I can certainly do the cutting and the glueing," I said. "Put her back on the phone and I'll tell her we can do it on the weekend."

"We'll come over to your place tonight," Kelly said. "The weekend is no good—Megan has to have her project to school by Thursday."

"By Thursday? But—but this is already Tuesday," I said. "How are we ever going to have a harp built and ready for school on Thursday?"

"I know, that's what Megan asked me, and I told her not to worry, that Pa could do anything."

"Well, you know, I was . . ."—I started to say as I struggled to find the right words—"I was just saying to Nanna that I wished I had something to do for the next two days."

And so, true to form, I cleared my schedule, for I knew that nothing could ever be as important as building my first harp, with my granddaughter.

Half an hour later the gang arrived. Nanna cleared the table while Megan and I pulled up our chairs and sat down. It was time to get to work. Megan was all business. She brought out the piece of paper and laid it on the table in front of us. It was a piece of plain white bond, eight-and-a-half inches wide and eleven inches long. Megan had made the only marks on the paper; she had drawn a harp. I smiled happily as I stared at her drawing.

"Well, there's no doubt about it. That's a harp all right," I said, as we both studied her drawing.

161

I have no idea what she was thinking, but for a few moments my mind wandered, and I forgot what the objective was; instead I found myself tracing around the outline of the harp with my finger, marveling at her artistic abilities. The harp on the paper was absolutely perfect. Then she looked up at me, and I realized that she was waiting for me.

"Oh, right, is — is this the size of the harp you want?" I asked Megan who was now looking at my finger as it continued to follow the lines on the paper.

"Well, it could be a little bigger, but we didn't have any bigger paper."

"Does this harp have to make music?" I asked.

"Uh-huh. Everybody has to play their instrument in front of the class."

"I see, so this harp does have to make a sound. Well then, I agree with you, buddy, I think your harp should be a little bit bigger, too," I said.

"Okay." And Megan looked up and gave her Mom a happy little smile that seemed to imply something that I had not been privy to.

"Do you have enough wood, Dad, or will you have to go and get some?" Kelly asked.

"Oh, he has lots of wood downstairs in his junk hole," Nanna chirped up. "I'm sure he'll find whatever he needs in all that garbage he has."

The "junk hole", as my loving wife referred to it, was actually my workshop; and the "garbage" was an assortment of valuable odds and ends and pieces of wood that were left over from previous projects.

"Hey!" I quickly interjected. "That's my workshop.

It may be garbage to some folks, but to me it's a treasure trove. I just have to find the right use for each little treasure that's down there."

"Do you have glue, to put some of that treasure together in the shape of a harp, Dad?" Kelly asked, changing the subject. After all, she had been around when Mar and I had gone down this road many times in the past. "I can go and get you some glue."

"Oh, I'm sure he has enough glue to stick all that garbage together," Mar said, and both she and Kelly laughed.

"We won't be using any glue, will we, Megan?" I said. "This is Megan and Pa's project — Mom and Nanna don't know what they're talking about, do they?"

"Uh . . .," Megan started to say with a degree of uncertainty as she looked at her mother. "They don't?" It was more of a question than a statement.

"You're not using glue?" Kelly asked and looked surprised. "How will you get the pieces to hold together?"

"I don't think that we'll need any glue to hold Megan's harp together, because there won't be any pieces," I said and winked at Megan. "We'd only have to use glue if we used separate pieces of wood for each side of the harp, and glued corners would only weaken the harp. It would be flimsy and not very strong. Megan and I are going to build her a harp that will be very strong and sturdy. We're going to build it out of one piece of plywood. Aren't we Megan?"

"I guess so," Megan said, and she gave her Mom a little questioning smile.

163

"You see, Megan?" Kelly said. "I told you Pa could do it. He can build anything—he just pretends he doesn't know how."

Then Megan and I went down into the basement. There we rummaged through the so-called garbage pile, as Nanna had so rudely labeled it. It didn't take long before we found what we were looking for—a piece of three-quarter-inch G1S fir plywood. It was a scrap of wood about three feet square.

"What do you think, buddy," I asked Megan. "Can you see a harp in this old piece of wood?"

Megan looked at it very carefully. She even got down and looked at it closely, as if she were scanning the surface, looking for a hint of the outline of her harp. She seemed to be unconvinced. And then it dawned on me. Nanna had already labelled all my lumber as garbage, and I realized that there never would be a harp in that old piece of plywood, or any other I had. I broke the silence.

"You know, Megan, now that I've had a real good look at this piece of garbage, I don't think there is a harp in it. What do you think, buddy, do you see a harp in this old valuable piece of wood?"

"I don't think so," she said, but she was still looking pretty hard at that piece of plywood.

"You know, buddy, I think that maybe Nanna was right—this is just a pile of garbage down here. What do you say we go to the lumber store and find us a piece of wood with a harp in it?"

"Okay," she replied.

Megan and I travelled down to the nearest lumber

store and found the plywood section. I pulled half a dozen pieces of plywood out of the bin. Megan gave each piece a very careful, thorough look, and she ran her finger over each piece, but that darn old harp just wasn't in any of them. Then I pulled out a very good-looking piece of plywood.

"By gosh, you know, buddy, I think I see that harp right here in this piece of plywood," I said. "I can almost hear it asking us to get our saw and set it free. Can you see the harp, buddy?"

She looked at that piece of wood very carefully and then at me. She wasn't convinced.

"I think we were looking at that piece of wood all wrong," I said. I turned it on end. "There, now, I think that your harp is sitting right in here, like this." Then, with my finger, I slowly traced out what I hoped was the outline of a harp. "Can you see it?" I asked.

Megan looked at that board for a few more seconds before answering.

"Uh-huh, but I think the top of the harp should be higher," she said and looked at me questioningly.

It was becoming obvious that Megan knew a whole lot more about harps than I did.

"By gosh, I think you're right, buddy," I said, and I smiled proudly as I had another look at that nice smooth, clean piece of plywood. "I can see it now, the top of the harp is definitely higher. I must have run my finger along the inside of the harp."

"Should we take this board?" I asked.

"Okay," she replied.

Back in my workshop, I quickly discovered that one

area where Megan didn't need my help was in sketching out the shape of the harp. She got down on that piece of plywood with a pencil and in no time flat she had the outside perimeter of the harp drawn. And she had been right, the top of the harp was considerably higher than I originally thought it was. Next she straightened up the edges of the lines with a straight edge. The outside perimeter of the harp was complete. Then she measured one-and-a-half inches all the way around the inside of the harp. When this was done, we could both see the harp where it lay nestled in its bed of plywood.

Using the saw was a little dangerous, so while Megan held the plywood for me, to keep it from moving, I used my jigsaw to cut along the lines that Megan had drawn. When I finished, the harp that Megan had seen in the plywood had been set free. We both paused to admire it.

Then Megan measured and marked out the holes along the shorter sides of the harp where the strings were to go, and I drilled little holes at each mark. The next step was harder and time-consuming, but Megan attacked it with vigour. She used a piece of sandpaper to sand every inch of that harp, inside and outside, until the edges were nice and smooth. Into each hole I inserted a #8 one-and-a-half-inch stainless steel screw. Megan screwed each one in as far as she could. When she was done, there were twenty screws, ten along each of the shortest arms of the harp.

For strings, I used different weights of monofilament line. I attached one end of a length of mono line to a screw and the other end to the matching screw on the other side. When all the mono lines were attached, each line could be tightened or relaxed by simply screwing the screw in or out. With the harp-stringing complete, Megan carefully tested each mono line, one at a time. A smile lit up her face when she was satisfied that each one would make its own distinct sound when she plucked it.

When the drawing, cutting, drilling, sanding and screwing were done, Megan and I removed the screws and the strings, and she painted her harp a bright green colour. Long before bedtime, Megan's harp was down in Pa's junk room waiting for the paint to dry.

On Wednesday, Megan and I replaced the screws and strings into the proper holes, and that evening after everyone had admired Megan's harp, we adjourned to the family room. Everyone, that is, but Megan. She stayed in the kitchen, adjusting the tension on the strings of her harp. The occasional plink on a string could be heard as she tested each for sound while she played with her special school project, the bright green harp.

Suddenly the room was filled with the sweetest sound I think I ever heard. Megan had somehow tuned her harp, and the sound was coming from the strings of the harp as she plucked them. And it was not a random plucking.

I stood up and looked. I couldn't believe my ears or my eyes. There sat Megan, beside the kitchen table. She had the bright green harp in front of her, and not only did it work, but she was making music with the darn

167

thing. Megan was actually plucking the cords on that little harp. This wasn't just a grandfather's wishful thinking. Megan was making music — the unmistakable tune of *Twinkle, Twinkle, Little Star* filled our house.

I stood there, a very proud grandfather ready to pop the buttons off my shirt, and each time she plucked a cord it tugged a string to my heart. I choked back the lump in my throat, and wiped a tear from my eye. I knew at that moment, when you combined a little girl's imagination and a grandfather's know-how, a wooden harp beat a Kleenex-box guitar by a country mile.

No wonder harps are always pictured in heavenly scenes. Here, in our house, at our table, sat an angel plucking her own little bright green harp.

obviously the only one who was in the dark. It's sometimes hard to face the fact that grandchildren do grow up.

"They're selling kettle corn for her," Kelly replied.

"Kettle corn!" I blurted out.

"Yeah, Dad, kettle corn," Kelly replied shaking her head — an obvious sign of frustration. "What's wrong with that?"

"Please don't tell me you're letting those two little girls go out by themselves where they're making that kettle corn," I said, and a sick feeling swept over me.

"They're fine, Dad," Kelly said. She seemed to be somewhat taken aback by my little outburst. "It's only kettle corn. Why are you getting so worked up?"

"Only kettle corn!" I snorted in disgust. "Did you check out how they make kettle corn before you let them go out there?"

I was having an instant flashback of my first and only encounter with kettle corn, an unforgettable chance meeting with a street vendor.

*   *   *   *   *

It all started out very innocently on a trip to Seattle, where I was going with Bill, my son-in-law, to see a Mariners baseball game. The Mariners were playing a home game against the San Francisco Giants and Barry Bonds, who was on a tear was hitting everything thrown at him out of the ballpark.

We had started out well in advance of the opening pitch. There was no way we were going to be late. In fact, we were even earlier than planned, a fortunate thing for us as it turned out. Long before we arrived at the stadium, we discovered that there was construction all over the place. Roads were blocked off, barricades were everywhere, and parking near the stadium was non-existent. Bill never complained. He inched that rental car around barricades and through alleys, dodging potholes and people, until he finally found a parking lot with available stalls. I'm sure that it was several miles from the baseball stadium. Although it was going to be a long walk, I thought we were still just a tad early to get into the stadium.

"What say we stop and grab a bite to eat before the game?" I said to Bill. "My treat."

"I thought I'd get a beer and a hot dog at the game," Bill replied. "We could have that for lunch. I'd like to see Barry Bonds take batting practice."

"I see. So you'd rather watch Bonds swat a few 'taters' than eat?"

"I always like to watch batting practice," Bill replied.

"That's why you're a true sports fan," I said. "You see, I never would have thought of giving up lunch for batting practice."

We continued to work our way through the maze, a regular obstacle course, this time walking to the stadium. It seemed as if we walked and walked, and all the while my hunger continued to grow. My poor old feet, which are great exaggerators, told me that we had been walking forever, and the stadium did not appear to be getting any closer than when we started. However, all was not lost — somewhere on our route we got lucky and stumbled across a vendor hawking huge bags of popcorn. It was like an oasis in the desert.

had increased his step. He was motoring along at a brisk pace. Meanwhile, I was busy shovelling kettle corn into my face as I followed along about a dozen long strides behind him.

The kettle corn vendor was right, the route to the Dude making the kettle corn and the stadium did lie straight ahead. At the end of a block, just before the stadium, tucked off into a little vacant space, we spotted the shirtless Dude making the kettle corn. I was fascinated as soon as I spotted him, and I had to stop and check it out. But it was not the Dude or his kettle corn that attracted me; it was the cauldron I had to check out. It had been years since I had seen anything like it. The cauldron was huge; it was about as large as the one my grandfather had once used to boil the slop that he fed to his hogs. Beneath the cauldron, instead of the wood fire my grandfather had used for heat, the Dude used propane. The propane fire roared and huge flames belched from underneath the cauldron and licked up its charred black sides.

"Hold on, Bill, I just want to watch this for a minute," I said.

"Barry Bonds is up," he protested, but he reluctantly stopped.

We were just in time to see the Dude, and he was one huge Dude. He had to weigh at least three hundred and fifty—no, maybe four hundred pounds. I could only stare at the huge Dude and his equally huge cauldron. I watched as the Dude hoisted his monstrous frame off a rusty old five-gallon gas drum that was pulled up close beside the cauldron. He grabbed a jug of oil and emptied it into the cauldron; then he threw several scoops of sugar into the oil before he picked up a bag and poured the contents — kernels of corn — into the mixture. He picked up a paddle; I would have bet anything it was big enough to be used on one of those old Viking ships. I know it was the biggest paddle I had ever seen. He waddled two small steps up to the cauldron. I winced, for I was sure that his huge belly was going to touch the side of the cauldron, but he had obviously performed this task many times. He stopped when his belly was only a fraction of an inch from being fried. He leaned over and stretched his arms out, out over the cauldron that was beginning to smoke, out as far as they would reach. Then, just as my grandfather had done many years before, he drove that paddle deep into the cauldron and began to stir the contents.

The big man attacked the kettle of corn like a man possessed. As the kernels began to explode, he worked faster, plunging that paddle into the popping kernels, stirring them violently. Again and again he drove that paddle home. He was putting on a real show. There were kernels of popped corn and there were kernels of unpopped corn flying in all directions. I saw one unpopped kernel fly out of the cauldron — straight as an arrow it went and nailed the big Dude right on his exposed belly. I could almost hear the flesh sizzle as the kernel stuck right where it hit. He grunted and his belly rippled. He dropped the paddle and using both hands he swatted the kernel, sending it flying into the crowd. Everyone watching knew that one stung, and we all winced as if we too felt the pain. But it didn't deter the

177

ROBERT J. (B0B) ADAMS

Bob Adams was born in Turner Valley, Alberta in 1938. He grew up in the Edson area, in a log house, built by his father on a farm rich in swamp spruce, tamarack, willows and muskeg.

Bob, an avid outdoorsman, was one of the fortunate few who was able to live his boyhood dreams as he entered the workforce. In 1960, after a number of years with the Alberta Forest Service and Royal Canadian Mounted Police, he began a career with the Provincial Government as a Fish and Wildlife Officer. For the next 33 years, he found his homes to include Brooks, Strathmore, Hinton, Calgary, Peace River and Edmonton.

In 1993, after a full career in Enforcement, he retired from Fish and Wildlife and wrote his first book, The Stump Farm. Today, Bob resides in Edmonton, Alberta with his wife Martha where he continues to work on his writing.